HELLO, I LOVE YOU

HELLO, I LOVE YOU
TED KLUCK

ADVENTURES IN ADOPTIVE FATHERHOOD

MOODY PUBLISHERS

CHICAGO

All Scripture quotations, unless otherwise indicated, are taken from *The Holy Bible,
New International Version®*, NIV®. Copyright© 1973, 1978, 1984 by Biblica, Inc.™
Used by permission of Zondervan. All rights reserved worldwide.

Scripture quotations marked ESV are taken from *The Holy Bible, English Standard
Version*. Copyright © 2000, 2001 by Crossway Bibles, a division of Good News Publishers. Used by permission. All rights reserved.

Published in association with the literary agency of Wolgemuth & Associates, Inc.

Edited by Elizabeth Cody Newenhuyse
Cover design and Image: Studio Gearbox
Interior design: Smartt Guys Design

Library of Congress Cataloging-in-Publication Data

Kluck, Ted.
  Hello, I love you : adventures in adoptive fatherhood / Ted Kluck.
    p. cm.
  Includes bibliographical references.
  ISBN 978-0-8024-5835-3
  1. Adoption. 2. Fatherhood. 3. Kluck, Ted. I. Title.
  HV875.K593 2010
  362.734--dc22

                              2010002317

This book is printed on acid free recycled paper containing 30% PCW
(Post Consumer Waste) and manufactured in the United States of
America by Bethany Press.

We hope you enjoy this book from Moody Publishers. Our goal is to provide high-
quality, thought-provoking books and products that connect truth to your real needs
and challenges. For more information on other books and products written and produced from a biblical perspective, go to www.moodypublishers.com or write to:

Moody Publishers
820 N. LaSalle Boulevard
Chicago, IL 60610

1 3 5 7 9 10 8 6 4 2

Printed in the United States of America

For my sons Tristan Volodymyr Kluck
and Maximilian Dmitri Kluck,
for the widows and orphans of Music Mission Kiev,
and for the hope of Anastasia.

CONTENTS

I guess I've still got a lot of healing to do.
— Francis L. Whitman, *The Darjeeling Limited*

The only true currency in this bankrupt world . . . is what you share with someone else when you're uncool.
—Lester Bangs, *Almost Famous*

INTRODUCTION

Can I share something with you, reader? It's something that may, in your eyes, make me profoundly uncool. I discovered something very important about myself during the writing of this book, and the process of two adoptions. That is, there are people who enjoy traveling to different cultures—these are the people from whom you receive enthusiastic, breathless letters and postcards featuring those people standing in front of this or that, or describing all of the wonderfully weird foods they've eaten. I'm not really one of those people, most of the time, despite my best of intentions, and despite really wanting to be one of those people.

There it is. It feels good to talk about it.

There are also evangelicals in our culture who have traveled to several continents and back before they've finished puberty. In fact, these days you're nothing if you haven't done several overseas jaunts by the end of college. We're raising a generation of expert fundraisers. I'm not one of those evangelicals. I grew up in a town of seven thousand people in the middle of a cornfield in Indiana and, the thing is, I *loved* it. I didn't go anywhere during college, as I graduated (1998) shortly before the "go everywhere" boom really took off.

This book is the story of two Ukrainian adoptions, told from the perspective of a father who desperately wanted children, who felt called to adopt orphans, but who struggled to enjoy the process. In trying to read about adoptions before our trip, I noticed that adoption books generally fell into two categories—cold, "how-to" type books; and sentimental narratives, some of which were quite good. This book began as a journal—some spiral-bound notebooks that came with me to Ukraine the first time, and which contained letters that I wrote to Tristan during the experience. In the first half of the book, it reads like I'm addressing Tristan directly, while the second half is a more straightforward narrative of Dima's adoption. They're both love letters to my boys, and the whole thing is a love letter to Kristin, my wife.

The book also, incidentally, contains two near-death experiences—one involving a SWAT team and the other involving some bare wires in an apartment in Kiev.

You'll also notice lots of frank, often sarcastic, prose about cultural differences—usually with the author as the punch line, as it was my inability to deal with these differences that provided a lot of humor (in retrospect) and anger (at the time). So if you're from Ukraine, don't hate me for pointing out these differences, and if you were part of the group that helped us adopt our children in Ukraine, know that we're forever grateful. As we say in America, "It's not you, it's me."

There's also some tough content regarding infertility. If this is something you've struggled with in your marriage, I hope this chapter encourages you, and I hope you feel less alone in your struggle. If you've been blessed with biological children, please don't feel guilty for having them, or in any way judged or made fun of by the observations in that chapter (see also: It not being you, but me).

Finally, the book contains lots of stories of God's faithfulness— stories that we thought were too meaningful not to be told. Little "piles of stones" along the way that remind us of God's goodness, love, and faithfulness. We hope that you'll read them and not only be entertained, but be motivated to think of Christ and our adoption as His sons and daughters. It is only the love of Christ, and our hope in Him, that got us through the first, the most difficult adoption in the history of our agency's work with Ukraine, then infertility, and finally a second adoption. And it was these adoptions, more than any other event or events in our lives, that truly taught us to find our peace, comfort, and identity in Christ.

PART 1

Tristan

My heart was going boom boom boom;

Son, he said, grab your things, I've come to take you home.

— Peter Gabriel, *Solsbury Hill*

CHAPTER 1:
THE PRICE OF LOVE

December 2003. Simferopol, Ukraine

I knew from the knock on the door that this wasn't an old babushka dropping by to trade borscht recipes. It wasn't a knock, really, but more of a pound. I looked out the peephole and found three large, angry Ukrainian men in full riot gear, with their guns trained on my forehead.

My options weren't great. Pretend I'm not here (bad, they'll come in anyway and probably break Milla and Sascha's door down in the process), or open the door and begin pleading in my six-word Russian vocabulary for them to please spare the lives of a cute, young American girl and her idiot husband who couldn't manage to properly program the old-fashioned security system that protects this flat which is in a building with about five hundred flats exactly like it.

Before Milla (a kind, gracious grandmotherly type who speaks about six words of English but kisses me on the cheek a lot) left for the orphanage where she is a physician, she explained how to program the system that would protect us and our suitcases full of cash and American snacks. The explanation involved a lot of numbers and a sequence that included locking and unlocking the deadbolt. I asked a few follow-up questions. I thought I knew what I was doing. I nodded and smiled a lot, and then swallowed hard before entering the numbers on the keypad. And this isn't the type of space-age keypad you see in movies or even American security-system commercials where well-dressed middle-aged white women punch in numbers before feeling secure at night. This is an old-school keypad.

The pounding at the door interrupted a morning composed of waiting for Simferopol to turn on the water (this, after several mornings of me standing naked in a cold bathroom before realizing that the city turns off the water for a while every morning), watching soccer on "Euro-Sport" (note: I hate soccer), and eating a Snickers for breakfast with a bottle of Coke, Sprite, or Fanta (the only three choices here). All of this while waiting for the best part of our day—the afternoon ride in the backseat of a tiny Moskvich, through old town and the open-air markets to the orphanage, to see Tristan, our soon-to-be son.

Just before the cops burst through the open door I encourage Kristin to stay seated in our bedroom—I don't want her to see her husband, in his pajama bottoms and Indiana University sweatshirt, take a hollow-point in the ear hole. I grab my passport and put my hands in the air, just like in the movies. Do I feel lucky, punk? Do reformers feel lucky or just foreordained? I pray for God's protection for my wife and, honestly, for me. These cops look mean (see: crewcuts) and maladjusted. I didn't figure that my first opportunity to see a machine gun in person would involve one being pointed at my forehead. And in Eastern Europe the cops don't come roaring up to the building in multiple police cruisers with sirens blaring, rather, they drive one little compact and pile into it, clown style.

Struggling writer Ted Kluck, 27, dies unexpectedly in a Ukrainian apartment, holding a half-eaten candy bar and a bottle of Coke Light. He is best known for a few pieces of snarky sports-satire that ran on ESPN.com and were forgotten shortly after they were published. Kluck is survived by his lovely wife, who will soon be remarrying a man who is funnier, more spiritual, and a better writer, and who also knows how to do things like program a security system.

After opening the front door, I gesture at the security system and eventually the cops put their guns down. Their hollering in Russian (really scary) eventually turns to muttering in Russian (less scary), as they pad through the little apartment and rifle through our suitcases a little bit. I'm convinced that what's left of our cash is a goner. These goons will be eating steak tonight on what was supposed to cover a round of medicine at the orphanage and our plane tickets home. We're in big trouble.

In this situation John McClane (the Bruce Willis character in *Die Hard*) would open up a floorboard and crawl into some ductwork where he would find a nine-millimeter and a cigarette lighter taped to the inside of the air shaft. He would then creatively whack the three goons and rifle through their backpacks where he would find enough money to fund another sibling group adoption. Unfortunately I'm not John McClane, and this is very, very real life. I would probably burn myself with the lighter and then get stuck crawling (awkwardly) in the dirty air shaft (*struggling writer, 27, dies in air shaft*). I settle on the John Piper approach and just pray like there's no tomorrow, which there may actually not be.

> *Dear Tristan,*
>
> *I almost became a 50 Cent lyric this afternoon—"Wear a vest without a gat, you's a target, Jack."*
>
> *The Ukrainian cops will tell this story down at the precinct later this afternoon, or whatever they call the precinct here. The story will be peppered with witty one-liners, just like in cop shows. Radios will crackle. Backup will be called for.*
>
> *Love,*
>
> *Dad*

We show them our adoption papers and finally, after some additional muttering, they leave our money alone and take their huge clunky boots, Kevlar vests, and assault rifles out of the flat. Pretty soon it's quiet again in the apartment and the only sound we hear is our own breathing and the sound of kids playing soccer on the dirt patch in front of the building. These are the kids who don't need an Astroturf field in a "Sports Complex" to be good at soccer, and their "soccer moms" are sitting in kiosks selling cigarettes or brooms to make ends meet. We thank God for our lives, the fact that the water is running and warm in the bathroom, and that we will get to see Tristan later in the afternoon.

When I walk out of the building to meet our driver for the trip to the orphanage, I put my hands behind my head like a felon. Sasha (different Sasha) thinks this is hilarious. This Sasha is about fifty years old but huge, with fists the size of hams. He looks like a former Russian shot-putter who could take a man apart in a fistfight in about thirty seconds. Ha ha. Gold teeth. He laughs out loud.

I always knock 'em dead here. Thank you, and good night. You've been a great audience.

□ □ □

ABOUT A YEAR AND A HALF BEFORE THE GUN INCIDENT

Dear Tristan,

You were conceived at a minor-league hockey game. Not exactly, but you know what I mean.

It was a year and a half ago about this time and your mother and I—man, that sounds so adult—went to Port Huron, Michigan, for a weekend to "sort some things out," because that's what college-educated people who have been married for several years call making life decisions. We sort things out.

More accurately, though, the idea for you was conceived about five years ago on a cold night in Lithuania. We visited an orphanage there that was a lot like yours. The kids were beautiful and wanted so badly to be loved. We loved them, for a night, and then we got into a van and cried. It hurt like crazy. We wanted to help but didn't know how.

So naturally, when I didn't know what to do about kids and growing our family, I took Mom to a minor-league hockey game—complete with the Zamboni, violence, and organ music. Your old man is a hopeless romantic.

The Port Huron Beacons were playing the Missouri River Otters, and Wayne Gretzky's kid brother Brent was playing out the end of his career with the Beacons. I'll tell you more about Gretzky later, when you get a little bit older. The arena was an ugly old concrete bunker in downtown Port Huron—it's the kind of place that gets the moniker "war memorial arena" or something like that. Stadiums always make me think of my dad. That night I was thinking of being a dad.

When you're thinking about being a father you start noticing things. You notice little kids at ballparks with their dads and—whereas before you didn't notice or care—now it almost brings you to tears for some reason.

After the game we went to our little hotel room and prayed. We prayed for you and about you, and then, finally, we decided to come get you.

Love, Dad

We've risked life and limb, trekking through the Michigan-in-February snow/sleet and the Detroit suburbs to get here. A word about the Detroit suburbs. They're horrible. In Chicago they at least dapple the outsides of the buildings in places like Oak Brook, Plainfield, and Wheaton with faux brick, faux awnings, and faux shingles. In Detroit it's just miles and miles of concrete, traffic, and neon.

But there's only so much you can get from a brochure and an informational mailing, so we skid the little Toyota Echo (which seems to weigh about twenty-six pounds, without us in it) in front of a low-slung brick building in Madison Heights. As I mentioned before, it's winter in Michigan so it got dark at about 4:58 p.m., creating an almost Scandinavian level of sun-deprivation. In the Northeast they call it SAD—Seasonal Affective Disorder. In the upper Midwest they call it "people getting really cranky." I've already cussed out a number of metro-Detroiters on the highway, which does little to calm my wife down. She and I deal with stress differently. She gets quiet and contemplative, while I invoke my inner dockworker and say things I regret later.

The inside of the building does little to put us at ease. There is the usual lonely, sad, "we had to get these for the meeting" plate of untouched cookies and sweaty cheese blocks. We enter a white-walled room to find lots of other awkward couples just like us. They are pretending to look through materials, waiting for the meeting to start. Normally, my wife and I would be nervous-talking at this point, but the place is stone silent.

Finally a woman representing Bethany Christian Services approaches. As this is a Christian meeting I expect a little bit of get-to-know-you banter. Perhaps an icebreaker à la church camp (*"My name is Ted and something you may not know about me is that I broke my collarbone playing semipro football with ex-convicts"*). There is none. Soon she is talking us through a document laying out the costs and wait times associated with adopting from different countries. The numbers are big. Real big. And the wait times are long. She is humorless, and I soon realize this is one of those "weed out the pretenders" meetings. The one where you go home feeling overwhelmed, and if you mail back the response card in a couple of days they'll know you are really serious.

We're in the somewhat unique position of choosing to adopt our first child because we felt called (read: wanted) to adopt, as opposed to being infertile (more on this little hubristic flourish later—it would come back to bite us). These are the kinds of decisions a couple makes when they are young, idealistic, and don't have a drop of analytical sense between them (we both majored in communications and neither of us can balance a checkbook).

We visited an orphanage back in the late 1990s, when we were serving a one-year missions stint in Lithuania. These are the kinds of short-term missions "experiences" that young Christians often have postcollege. It's a "find yourself" type of deal. A nice, experienced missions family takes you under their wing while you struggle with theology and free will versus God's sovereignty (and graduate school versus dad's company versus mission work), and say things like "I'm not sure what God wants me to do with my life" and they say things like "I know what you mean . . . let's take a taxi to the McDonald's in Vilnius and eat six Big Macs, and then go home and watch American DVDs." You write a monthly prayer letter about all that you're learning and all the cool cathedrals, old-world European cities, and historic landmarks you're seeing which, I'm sure, is really annoying to all of the good, hardworking people who are supporting you but who have never been to Europe.

There was one thing, though, that really blew my mind about Vilnius: the orphanages full of beautiful, needy kids. When a country's economy is in the toilet, and joblessness and hopelessness are rampant (see: Michigan, currently), people don't necessarily stop having kids. Hence these orphanages were seemingly on every street corner and were all varying degrees of horrible. We piled in a van one night and went to one of these places to play

American games, sing American songs, and bring American food to the kids. I was nervous beforehand. I didn't want to feel sad, but I knew I would. It's sort of like trying to get into the mood to watch *Schindler's List*—you know it's going to be good for you, but you just don't want to.

The kids there were so open, so sweet, and so eager for our attention. It was as if this one little evening out of our entire long, affluent lives was the greatest thing anyone had ever done for them. There were children there of all ages—little babies in cribs, toddlers, grade school-age kids, and even teenagers. There were two in particular—a girl around fourteen or fifteen, and a baby who captured our hearts. But there was nothing we could do, really. The girl begged us in her broken English to adopt her. We gave her our hats, bracelets, and necklaces and vowed to call and visit again.

We went home to our chilly Vilnius flat that night—exhausted and high from the excitement of spending an evening playing and being surrounded by an eager group of adoring children—and bawled our eyes out. We had no idea on earth what to do when confronted with needs on such a large scale. We were young (early twenties), naïve, and idealistic, and wanted to save each and every one of those children but were acutely aware that we had just abandoned them again.

So we prayed, and vowed—like people in their early twenties always vow—that we would Do Something about the hundreds, thousands, of children in Eastern European orphanages. We had no idea what we would do, but the idea was there. And, for the record, we never made it back to the orphanage.

By the summer of 2002 we had been married for six years and needed an answer to the "when are you going to have kids" question that was increasing in both frequency and intensity. It's amazing that people who may be afraid to discuss religion or politics are perfectly comfortable asking you about your reproductive plans and habits.

We had been thinking about kids a lot. Among our biggest concerns about parenthood was our ability to be good parents—you know, unselfish, responsible, financially sound and all of the other nebulous qualities we always associated with mature older people. Whenever we thought about kids we thought about adoption. It just made so much sense on a practical level, a spiritual level, and an emotional level.

As we talked and prayed about it more and more, we fell in love with the idea and felt total peace about it. We felt that if we could only have a child one way—birth or adoption—that we would be missing out on something if we chose not to adopt. And that summer—while we were "up North" swimming and praying and watching hockey, our future son was born on August 4 in Simferopol, Ukraine.

HOME STUDY

We live in an old house (1930s) in a ramshackle, blue-collar neighborhood in Lansing-proper. The neighborhood is run down in that while one house might feature a nicely manicured garden in which a kind elderly woman putters each afternoon, the next house might have a '79 Cadillac up on blocks in the front yard and several guys who look like they just stepped out of a Snoop Dogg video standing around drinking Boone's Farm out of paper bags.

For the record, it seems to have more of the latter. And our house is neither of these.

We bought the place when we were in our "incarnational-living/reach-out-to-the-inner-city" phase, a phase which lasted roughly a night until I realized I really liked the quiet. I missed the neighborhood I grew up in, where you left the doors unlocked fifty-one weeks of the year and only locked up when the County Fair and its "carnies" came to town. I feel like most young, white evangelicals go through this phase with varying degrees of success and sincerity. Call it white guilt or whatever. For us, it didn't take. It should also be noted that this house was all we could afford at the time and turned out to be, in spite of its shortcomings, something of a miracle. We bought it from some church acquaintances, and used the profit from our old place to finance the first half of the adoption.

Kristin has lit scented candles and tried to make the little dwelling as appealing and responsible-looking as possible for our home-study visit. We've both even gone to great lengths to put on cool-but-not-too-cool outfits. Yes, we're trying too hard. The home study is the step in the adoption process where the potential adoptive family gets a visit from the adoption agency in which the agency assesses the house and gets to know the prospective parents. Our bachelor's degrees in communication arts have been good for very little up to this point, but we're confident in our ability to put on a top-notch conversational performance for Jennifer. The house, however, is another story. We just hope our next-door neighbor doesn't pick tonight to get drunk and relieve himself off the back porch, as he has been known to do on occasion.

Kristin started the information-gathering process in earnest when we got back from our hockey/deciding-to-become-parents weekend. Meanwhile, Bethany Christian Services checked up on everything—our finances, our marriage, our childhoods, family relationships, job history, medical history, criminal record . . . it was exhaustive. We even got to take a trip down to the Office of Immigration in Detroit to be fingerprinted by the FBI in the kind of drab, depressing government building that makes even the grittiest parts of Eastern Europe look airy and inviting by comparison. We took a number and waited in plastic chairs for a while, and were shown a creepy-but-cool immigration documentary about the history of Ellis Island.

It should be added here that having the wrong caseworker can make or break a home study. Thankfully, we have the right caseworker—a young woman named Jennifer who doesn't seem to bat an eye at our ghetto neighborhood (relief). She takes a walk through the house and for the first time I see the tiny bedrooms, bright colors (when you live in a dark gray neighborhood it's important to have some color in your life), and surroundings through the eyes of another. I see the effort Kristin put into making this nondescript house in a nondescript blue-collar neighborhood a home, and it makes me proud. And I look forward to playing catch in the backyard and wrestling on the living room floor with our own child.

◻ ◻ ◻

It strikes me that in our neighborhood people are conceiving all the time. Fathers are impregnating and leaving. Young girls are making bad choices or, sadly, may not have choices in the matter. There are just lots of babies being made, and lots of people becoming "parents" without much foresight or "accidentally," so it seems odd that we should have such a rigorous application process to become parents ourselves, especially when there are so many children in need.

Which also speaks to the "why are you going halfway around the world and spending tens of thousands (more on that later) of dollars to adopt when there are a bunch of needy kids right in your neighborhood" question. It's a question we got from our parents, who rightfully were concerned about the price tag, but also about the prospects of us having to travel internationally again. They, understandably, didn't grow up in a generation where Christian kids all seem to have been on missions trips to Venezuela, Spring Break in Panama City, Bosnia, and South Africa all before getting their driver's licenses. Times have changed with regard to international travel and Christians, for better or worse. Evangelical parents now seem to spend a lot of time just trading fundraising letters and $200 contributions to their kids' mission experiences.

I'd like to say we spent many nights in prayer about this issue but, in reality, we prayed about it a few times and (hopefully) trusted the Lord to direct our feelings on the issue. And our feelings are that though there are many needy children in the Potter Park neighborhood in Lansing, we didn't necessarily want to be running into their biological mothers at Meijer on Saturday mornings (see: open adoptions). And we'd had friends who had been burned by the "get summoned to the hospital only to learn that after a rigorous evaluation process the seventeen−year−old birth mother has decided to keep her child" scenario, which sounds like a nightmare. Granted, some are called to this type of adoption, and we admire them. The biggest factor, though, was that we'd been to

Eastern Europe, and been told that the kids who weren't adopted usually became small-time criminals (boys) or prostitutes (girls) or both when they were released from the orphanage at age eighteen. The kids were usually deposited at the orphanages shortly after their birth but sometimes their parent would drop them off in early childhood, promising to come back and get them when they had a little bit more money, and never return.

○ ○ ○

After our first experience at the Bethany introductory meeting, we were a little worried about Jennifer. The adoption process is emotionally draining as it is, and I wasn't sure we could handle another "stern-taskmaster" type of night. Thankfully she is warm but businesslike, thorough and helpful, and we loved our sessions with her. God was so graciously evident in matching us with her.

We gave her the keys to our financial history, our personal lives, and our friends, several of whom kindly wrote "the Klucks will be great parents" letters at Bethany's request. And then we waited.

THE BANK

I feel like Henry Hill in *Goodfellas*. I wonder if I can have the cash placed in an empty briefcase, or a brown paper bag as I had seen done in so many gangster movies. I've worn dress pants and a tie because, as I was explaining to my wife that morning, people treat you better when you're wearing dress pants.

After receiving Bethany's stamp of approval on our ability to be parents (relief—thank You, Lord) we were informed that we were to withdraw $20,000 in cash and then wait for a call from Dr. Dubrovsky—a Russian medical doctor who heads up

Bethany's Ukrainian adoption program on the overseas end. This is about $19,950 more dollars than I have ever had in my pocket at any given time, and it will be used to fund apartments, cab rides, and meals in Ukraine, in addition to the Ukrainian government's adoption fees.

The majority of the proceeds from the sale of our first house have been spent on home study fees, and Bethany's adoption fees, so we'll have to be approved for a loan in order to walk out of the bank with twenty-large on our person. I walk to the window, nervous, and try to communicate this to a teller. She tells us to wait (again, with the waiting) and soon we are led through a labyrinth of gray cubicles (note: I'm glad I don't work in a place like this) to a woman who will (hopefully) get us closer to the cash.

We've come armed with about fifty pounds of paperwork explaining in detail each aspect of the adoption and every jot and tittle of our financial history. She clatters away on a keyboard for what seems like forever, while we sit awkwardly and try to look like the charming-but-responsible young couple.

"We can't do it," she says, suddenly. She thanks us for coming and then pauses. This is where we're supposed to get up and graciously exit the building without twenty grand in small bills. I no longer feel like Henry Hill from *Goodfellas*. I now feel like Woody Allen—small, thin, and anxious. Kristin is seething. I can see the steam coming out of her ears, and I can see her lower lip starting to quiver. She is unbelievable at keeping her cool through the day-to-day annoyances of life (traffic, long lines, family issues), whereas it is me who usually flips out several times per day. However, I'd like to think that I've learned to keep my wits about me when the big stuff goes down. I calmly ask the lady to please double-check and try again. She goes to check with someone else and no doubt do more typing. Kristin is crying.

"Do. Not. Worry. About. Your. Future," I tell her, invoking my best Jerry Maguire impersonation. "You and I are going to be . . . just fine." She laughs and wipes away a tear.

Dear Tris,

When your mom and I were dating we used to hang out together long into the night, and into the early hours of morning. Those wee hours—after Letterman and before the first SportsCenter. That's no-man's-land baby, no-man's-land.

I would kiss her good-bye at her door and then walk down the middle of the street in the pitch-blackness, with the mist already beginning to settle on the grass and cars. I felt like an old gunslinger. I owned the street. I felt like the world's greatest lover, and like I'd just won the lottery and not told anyone yet.

We could have used the lottery today, as getting you almost stalled at a bank in East Lansing. They mixed up some paperwork. Some ID numbers . . . some codes . . . a keystroke error . . . or whatever. You'll learn, unfortunately, that adult life is often a series of long lines, identification numbers, and keystroke errors. Moments where you feel like an old gunslinger are few and far between— unless you're Brett Favre (more on him later).

Love,
Dad

"I double-checked and the mistake was on our end," explains Bank Lady, smiling, her heels *click, click, click*ing out an official beat on the office tile. "You can go up front to the window to get your money." Kristin's tears of fear turn to little tears of joy. She's wrung out. What we don't realize is that we'll need to get used to these "near misses" as they will happen often in Europe. Only there we'll be hungry, tired, and sick.

We sign seventy-five more sheets of paper before walking to the front to collect the bills, which end up coming to us in two small envelopes—decidedly less cinematic and cool than the briefcase or brown paper bag. But we still smile at each other on the way out. We're going to Ukraine.

But our trip was different. It was a classic affirmation of everything right and true and decent in the national character. It was a gross, physical salute to the fantastic *possibilities* of life in this country—but only for those with true grit. And we were chock full of that.

— Hunter S. Thompson, *Fear and Loathing in Las Vegas*

CHAPTER 2:
LEAVING, ON A JET PLANE, NOT KNOWING WHEN WE'LL BE BACK AGAIN

Dear Tristan,

It's about 10 p.m. and we're in an airplane over the Atlantic Ocean. We're in the middle row, which is the worst place to be on a long flight—hemmed in on all sides by the flying public. But, as they say in sports, we're just happy to be here, and to be nearer to you.

Your mother is wrapped up in her little denim jacket watching a cartoon movie with the headphones on. She looks like a little girl right now. Your mother is a beautiful woman. Her face is so smooth and bright and I realize that in our seven years together she hasn't aged at all. I, on the other hand, keep finding gray hairs.

Reading a book by Don DeLillo right now—he writes like I do in my wildest dreams. Who would have thought *a hundred years ago that we'd be 20,000 feet in the air, reading books in steel tubes?*

Love,

Dad

We didn't have much time to prepare after getting The Call, but it couldn't have been more than a few days. After receiving the results of our home study, a one-sentence synopsis that cost about $6,000 and read something like "Ted and Kristin are approved for Ukrainian adoption and seek a child of either gender as young as possible but under five years old," we compiled the rest of the paperwork and waited a few months. One day the phone rang, and within a few days time we were on the plane.

I have the whole $20,000 in cash strapped around my waist in a little fabric pouch that works in the same way as a fanny pack but has a much lower profile and is worn underneath the clothing. This device was purchased at the request of Bethany Christian Services, and after some dialogue we decided I would wear the whole amount. I packed the fabric pouch the night before our flight left—money in the plastic baggies first, squeeze the air out, and then into the pouch and around the waist. Deep breath. After the 9/11 tragedy, everybody is a little skittish in airports, so I try to dress as "harmless and American" as possible so as not to get patted down through security where they really should buy you dinner first (belt off, shoes off, pat the waist, etc.). I'd just as soon not explain all of the cash strapped to my waist.

I've made many trips through the Detroit airport, a facility which is, really, a tale of two airports. The nonrenovated Delta terminal looks like the world's largest Greyhound station—a dimly lit hole strewn with garbage and smelling faintly of a mixture of Cinnabon, grade school, and industrial-grade cleaning agents. However, the Northwest terminal is a gleaming, well-lit, steel-and-glass structure that feels more like a mall than an airport terminal.

We are weighed down with luggage. To say that the length of our trip is nebulous would be an understatement. We've been told to be ready for anything from a week to thirty days, which came as a little bit of a surprise to my employer, who has been more than understanding. At this point I'm still toiling away as a fundraiser at a Big Ten university. It's a job that I struggle to like sometimes, which I'm sure comes as no surprise to anyone, including my employer, who knows that I want to write more than I want to help older alums part with their endowment dollars. Still, the job is the proverbial Golden Handcuff. It looked great on paper and has allowed us to adopt, which will make it hard to quit when that time comes.

We were told to pack for the cold, and for streets that would be poorly maintained and slushy—in other words not a whole lot different than Detroit. We've packed toys for the orphanage, medicines for our child and for ourselves, and lots of books. Like I said before, DeLillo will be my author of choice for this trip—however, depressing and postmodern might not be the way to go. I realize early on that I should have probably gone with something more uplifting. Like a John Grisham thriller, where good prevails and the guy gets the girl.

A word about drugs—bring something to help you sleep. I've just taken two Tylenol PM on the airplane and I might as well have downed a Red Bull or snorted a line of coke. I am jacked beyond belief and it will take more than an over-the-counter sleep aid to help me calm down. Perhaps something along the "horse tranquilizer" lines.

Transatlantic flights offer an interesting array of people to watch in the middle of the night when sleep is scarce. There is, of course, the Middle Eastern Guy who is dressed in a robe of some kind and has a beard which after 9/11 makes him look scary and ominous instead of just a run-of-the-mill awkwardly dressed Muslim. The real challenge on this trip, though, will come from the Greek National Water Skiing Team (seriously) who have been seated a row or two ahead of us. They look to have returned from some recent conquest in which they nailed all of their routines and won something, so now we're surrounded by twentyish swarthy men who are ready to party despite the late hour. Loud talk. Loud laughing. Drinks flowing. It's good to be a Greek water skier tonight and bad to be me. I imagine them flirting with my wife on their way to the WC (that's euro for bathroom) and I imagine myself beating the tar out of them. Nice.

Directly in front of us is a college girl (backpack, hoodie) who looks to be leaving the country for the first time in search of Life Experiences. She is a loud talker, so after an hour or so I learn that she is staying together with her boyfriend, her friend is keeping the baby, and she is, like, so excited to be going to Europe. Her inevitable union with the Greek Water Skiing team is not "if" but "when." I try not to think about it but my money is on it happening sometime before our short layover in Berlin.

○ ○ ○

No sleep. The Berlin airport is a blur, save for the fact that it is very modern and cold (think, stainless steel) and does nothing to dispel the notion that Germans (my heritage) are coldly efficient. Also, there's some sort of arty, barbed-wire motif going on around the trams that seems to me an odd choice.

◌ ◌ ◌

Tris,

Just slept for thirteen hours in our Ukrainian flat and I had four dreams about home—crazy dreams about Hartford City (my hometown), Taylor University, and the Indianapolis Colts. The last twenty-four hours were a whirlwind . . .

We were met on the airport tarmac (I like that word, tarmac) in Kiev by a terse man saying my name. He flashed a business card and said he was there to "move us through the process." He took our passports and raced to the front of the Passport Control line. Now I'm freaking out. I've been in Ukraine for roughly ten minutes, and I've already given my passport to a stranger.

"How much money do you have?" he asked.

"About $20,000," I replied, "for the adoption."

It felt really hot in the room and my head was spinning. The people looked comfortingly familiar—Eastern European women ranging from beautiful to babushka-with-moustache, and the men all efficiently smoking cigarettes.

"Adoption?" he asked. "Did you hire me?"

He then said something about "going out front to check" and scurried away. Ostensibly to go and find the

nearest three thugs in nylon sweatsuits who would be
glad to shove us into the trunk of a Lada (small, Russian
car) and help us part with our twenty-large. My bowels
felt like they were going to explode. And our best suitcase
was broken.

    More Later,
    Dad

◌ ◌ ◌

I mull my options and decide that first we need to fix our dete-riorating suitcase which must have been dropped from a twenty-story building, dragged behind a semitruck, and then "bent like Beckham" somewhere between Detroit and here. Kristin works her magic with a roll of yellow tape, and though I managed to get our passports back from Tarmac Guy, I figure we only have a few minutes before they catch up with us outside. And then there is the nagging realization that we haven't yet met our real Bethany Rep.

Me: "Was it supposed to be a guy or a girl?"

Kristin: "I don't know."

We've read eleven books about international adoption, packed every possible item of clothing or drugs for every possible travel contingency, yet we don't know the sex or name of our Bethany contact. Customs is easier than I thought it would be. They rifle through our bags, looking through the random assortment of toys, medicines, and clothing as though it were nothing remark-able.

As I begin to lug our gear through customs, out of the corner of my eye I see Kristin approaching a fashionable young woman. She is smiling and they embrace. "I'm Lesya," she says. "You must be Kristin." Exhale. I scan the room quickly for Tarmac, but he is nowhere in sight.

◻ ◻ ◻

Kiev is a huge city. Population-wise, at 2.7 million inhabitants, it's similar to Chicago and we seem to drive forever through miles and miles' worth of Soviet-era high-rise apartment complexes, and through sections of town where new, more Westernized high-rise complexes are going up. Our driver looks like Elvis Costello and chats amicably, happy to work on his English. His name is Sergei and I like him almost immediately.

> *Tristan,*
>
> *Elvis Costello is a musician whose name you will invoke when you're trying to appear cool. However, you'll notice pretty quickly that nobody ever plays their Elvis Costello records (see also: Tom Waits). I mean, they're never playing at anybody's house.*
>
> *Best,*
>
> *Dad*

Lesya wears a cellphone around her neck and it rings often. She barks orders into the phone every few minutes. These conversations all sound terse and chippy but we'll grow to realize that this is just how Lesya communicates. She could be any businesswoman, anywhere. Tight ponytail. Black slacks, and the type of pointy-toed elf shoes that are popular in Eastern Europe right now.

She takes us to an "American" market where we sleepwalk through some shopping and I buy "Kievas Cutletas" (chicken

Kiev) which are processed pieces of chicken shaped like actual drumsticks. We load up on bottled water (can't drink out of the tap) and make our way to the flat, which is in a really cool blue building in Kiev. We traverse the dark hallways (just like Vilnius) and are herded into a tiny elevator that whisks us up to the flat—a tidy one-bedroom with a nice view of the city skyline.

I feel an almost tangible sense of relief when I unstrap the money thing around my waist and count out the Benjamin Franklins, which represent Lesya's fee and that of our driver, Sergei. Lesya assures me again that I don't need to tip Sergei each time we ride in the car. This is included in our fee. The phone around Lesya's neck buzzes almost nonstop and soon she is out the door, with the money; and for the first time in forty-eight hours or so, we are alone.

◻ ◻ ◻

Dear Tristan,

3 a.m. in Kiev. Insomnia in any language is still insomnia. You think it will be different—more glamorous—in Europe, but you are wrong. You're still a guy pacing a room and failing to sleep. There are people in old-town villas outside your window with their lights off and you still burn with jealousy because they are sleeping and you aren't.

Still, there are similarities. You hear a train rumble by and think of the trains in your neighborhood. You hear the sound of Ukrainian television in the flat below, and instead of blaming the noise for keeping you up you're glad to have found an accomplice in sleeplessness. You wonder if the downstairs neighbor might like to talk.

The problem is that I have too much time on my hands for thought and reflection here. There is no 6:30 Seinfeld rerun on TBS, and no PlayStation in the attic to lull me into a false sense of security. I miss that. America is all about cultivating the false sense of security.

Today we successfully got lunch at an Italian restaurant in our neighborhood. We also went to the market and bought more supplies. It feels good to buy. To transact business. We feel a sense of accomplishment. Tomorrow we are going to the Ministry of Adoption to look at some files (on you, as it turns out) which is why I'm up half the night. Excited. Nervous. Prayerful (a little).

I prayed for good sleep tonight, but it didn't work. I guess God is not a cosmic sleep-aid.

Yours,

Dad

◯ ◯ ◯

Gave a few bucks to a homeless Ukrainian lady this morning, and then I saw her later in the afternoon sitting on the sidewalk drinking a beer with a huge smile on her face. It made me feel as good as I've felt in a long time.

◯ ◯ ◯

It's freezing in the Ministry of Adoption. In fact, there isn't much to it at all. We were led down an alley to a back staircase and into a dark hallway. I have my scarf wrapped tight around my neck, indoors. It's a wet, seepy, pervasive cold. As I understand this step in the process, we'll see some files here on different children, which we'll then have to choose from. This stresses us out, to say the least. We spent much of the night praying that God would make it abundantly clear which child we were to choose and, in fact, perhaps absolve us of having to choose altogether. This almost seems more than we can bear.

After what feels like forever, we're led into another dark office, where Lesya is engaged in more pointed dialogue with an older man with thick glasses sitting behind a desk. Her cellphone sways around her neck as she gestures and talks. We sit silently like kids in the principal's office. The man with the glasses produces two huge books full of, literally, files. This stuff isn't housed on computers, nor is it even in a filing cabinet. He begins flipping through the huge, dusty books. We see Polaroid pictures of babies and toddlers flying by, and the sensation is a little disconcerting. Lesya continues to dialogue on our behalf though we have no idea what she's saying.

"There is a child in Simferopol," she says finally. "Today is the first day he is available for adoption. His name is Volodymyr. The nurses say he is very clever, and very beautiful. A prince." She is smiling as she talks, though Guy Behind Desk looks like he could be renewing a license plate. He yawns. "Would you like to go and meet Volodymyr?" Lesya asks. We say yes and are informed that we will fly out tomorrow morning, on a small plane, to Simferopol, which (we had to look on a map) is in the Crimean peninsula.

Things happen very abruptly here. One moment you're patting yourself on the back for buying a roll of paper towels in Kiev, and the next moment you're on an airplane bound for somewhere else. There's not much time for mulling things over or preparing yourself. You get leaner and harder, you learn to move quickly and travel light.

Lesya says that the director favored us because we are so young, and gave us a child who is young (fourteen months) and "absolutely healthy."

We celebrate with a whirlwind tour of Kiev, knowing now that this is the last significant time we'll spend with Lesya and Co. in the city, save for a night or two in transit on the back end of the adoption process. She takes us to St. Sofia's and St. Michael's—beautiful old cathedrals—unlike anything in America, where "concrete bunker with plastic chairs" seems to be the prevailing church fashion of the day. These cathedrals aren't above making a buck, however, as they each have gift shops where we purchase a CD of Ukrainian Monk Chamber Music which I know before I've even collected my change will never actually be listened to by either of us.

After the tour we have lunch in a Kiev diner that is lined with Jeppesen aviation maps and other pieces of aviation detritus including parachutes hanging from the ceiling. This reminds me of sitting in my dad's office (he's a pilot) as a kid—looking at his maps. I wish he was here. He loves this kind of stuff. I wish he could meet his grandson with us tomorrow, or whenever it happens. The meal today is light and celebratory—Lesya feeling good about a job well done, and us feeling good because we can pray for our son by name. Little do I know I'll be back in this selfsame smoky diner in a couple of months, feeling like I'm on the brink of death.

◌ ◌ ◌

Our celebratory mood doesn't last long, as we take a phone call tonight from Lesya that throws the whole thing into question.

Simferopol is located in the Crimean peninsula which, oddly, though it is in Ukraine, operates under its own set of rigid, frustrating and generally inconvenient rules and regulations. According to Lesya the judge there is inflexible on the thirty-day hearing, which means we will have to return to America to wait thirty days before coming back to take custody.

"Can we bribe them?" I feel like a typical American as soon as these words leave my mouth. But I didn't come to Ukraine with twenty-large around my waist to spend it on stacking dolls and chanting-monk CDs. Let's get this thing done.

We can't bribe them, and the bad news continues when we find that we may have to wait an additional thirty days BEFORE our court date. Meaning a grand total of three trips and two months of waiting around before we can be home with our son. This, she tells us, is unprecedented. But she also tells us that much of what happens in Crimea is unprecedented.

The phone call leaves us with much to pray and agonize about, and not a whole lot of time to do it. We need to have a decision by morning, and it's already late night. Plane ride tomorrow to Crimea, or back to the Ministry of Adoption in the morning to find another child—one with fewer strings attached who isn't located in the Ukrainian capital of doing-things-the-hard-way. Included in the decision is the expense of traveling back to Ukraine three times, and the feeling like we're being taken advantage of by Crimea, and bilked out of more money, just because they hold all of the leverage and we're easy to rip off at this point.

We rant and rave against the system, and pray that God will help us to trust Him in this. He has come through over and over again, so we have to believe He'll do the same here. There will be no other child. Tristan (Volodymyr) has already been abandoned once, and we're not going to do it to him again.

◌ ◌ ◌

My first thought upon seeing this aircraft is that Frank Sinatra probably flew on this baby back in the Rat Pack days. The term "old school" doesn't adequately describe it. Think Humphrey Bogart in *Casablanca*. Silver fuselage. Tan drapes. Propellers, not jets. My breathing gets shallow and I focus very hard on trying not to hyperventilate.

We are hugged good-bye by Lesya and told that we will be met at the airport by a woman named Svetlana who will be our contact/interpreter/guide in Simferopol. I am sad to see the Ukraine team go. I had become comfortable with Lesya and Sergei who took us sightseeing and shopping in the Kiev markets.

On board, however, the trip takes a turn for the better when we are served—gasp—a real meal, something you don't see on an American airline flight unless you qualify for DoubleUltimatePlatinumGoldElite status and are in the air for over eleven hours. We are lucky to get the meal. It will be the last time we eat the rest of the day.

◌ ◌ ◌

Waiting. This will become, in many ways, the story of our trip to Simferopol. After being picked up at the airport by Svetlana (nice, older, matronly, a worrier) we rode into downtown Simferopol in the backseat of a Lada (think: the smallest car imaginable). We will spend a lot of time in the backseat of this Lada before it's all said and done. Our driver, Sasha, looks like he could kill me in about 2.5 seconds with his bare hands, and I'm a pretty big guy.

Svetlana is stressed out and "sick" over her three-year-old granddaughter who was taken to the hospital this morning. We're reminded that the people we meet here have more going on in their lives than simply collecting our cash and making things smooth for us. We wish we could communicate our concern for her somehow, and hope that she hears good news from her husband soon.

Simferopol is not unlike a gray, industrial American city along the lines of a Flint, Michigan. We drive past factories with pictures of Stalin painted on the side, and then finally into old town where we would wait for several hours in the backseat of the Lada outside a government building. We don't yet feel comfortable walking around, and each only have a Snickers in our backpack.

Dear Tristan,

We do a lot of waiting in dark hallways here, while people argue about us in a different language.

This town, Simferopol, with its crowded streets, makes Kiev look like the Taj Mahal. This place is bleak, man. It's Gary, Indiana or Metro Detroit. Sometimes it feels like dirty dishwater. I'd like to take a bar of soap and a weed whip to the whole place.

It's 4:00 and we haven't eaten since breakfast. Nobody eats lunch here. I'm gonna lose some weight here . . . in fact, I think I've already lost five pounds and would kill for a pizza right now.

I just saw a guy grab a half-smoked cigarette off a ledge and light it, looking like he'd just won the lottery.

That's poverty.
   Hope to Meet You Soon,
   Dad

◇ ◇ ◇

There is some confusion as to where we'll stay tonight, so we drive around Simferopol for what seems like forever. Our guide, Svetlana, is very kind and apologetic. We keep assuring her that it's okay, but look forward to settling into a bed somewhere—anywhere—for the night. There has been talk of us bunking in the apartment of another Ukrainian family—a woman who works at the orphanage and her husband. I'll be honest, this freaks me out a little bit. The only thing worse, in my opinion, than having overnight company is being an overnight guest somewhere.

We pull into a pizza parlor which, as it turns out, isn't too far away from the orphanage. By the end of the meal I'm feeling much better. It's good to be back. A little pizza and some tin-can techno music and suddenly I'm feeling like this whole crazy gig might actually work out. We might get out of this place with our sanity and a baby. We'll see.

Sasha finally pulls up (is this guy getting paid by the hour?) in front of the Hotel Mockva (Hotel Moscow) which, from the outside looks like a relatively decent place to lay our heads. Inside we get our keys (the real, metal kind, not pieces of programmed plastic) from a full-figured Russian lady right out of central casting, and find our room which, unfortunately, doesn't have a door that locks (see: keys, unnecessary). This after Svetlana told us to "lock your doors, because people like to prey on Americans." I slide a coffee table in front of the door and restrap what's left of our cash around my waist before taking the bed closest to the door. It's going to feel good to sleep.

◠ ◠ ◠

Dear Tristan,

We met you today, Son! They put you in my lap and you were so solid—so beautiful and strong. Your arms and legs felt like little tree trunks. You smiled when I squeezed the toy duck, and you didn't cry once—not even close. You're a tough kid to survive this hellhole. The hallways are dark and cave-like, and it seems like nobody turns on the lights in this country.

You played so well with your mother. Everybody says you two look alike. Must be the chubby cheeks. More later, buddy . . . we'll get you out of here soon.

Much, Much Love,

Dad

From the outside the orphanage looks like almost every other building in Ukraine, in that it features Soviet-era architecture (lots of gray brick) and the kind of distinctive Soviet-era windows that defy description, but that you intuitively know if you've traveled in one of these countries. The windows are amazing in their inability to block even a little bit of draft.

The hallways inside the orphanage are dark, and we're first led into what looks to be the nicest office in the place, occupied by the orphanage director. We shake hands and exchange a few pleasantries in broken languages. His office is filled with stuffed animals (kind of weird—why aren't these given to the kids?) and another Soviet-era staple—furniture that looks really nice but isn't actually comfortable in any way.

From there it's upstairs to another dark office to meet with a doctor who will give us a rundown on our son's medical conditions. She's a young woman, and we can immediately tell that she's very kind, though it's difficult to communicate across the language barrier. She smiles frequently and makes good eye contact, and for the first time that day our nerves give way to ease. She tells us that although there is a heart condition listed on Tristan's file, these are often indicated as a way to get healthy children eligible for adoption, and while it is probably nothing we should get it checked out stateside just to be safe. She also explains that there has been a round of pneumonia going around the orphanage—though we can't ascertain if this is the type of pneumonia that can kill you, or if they're just using that word to describe a cold or strep throat. "We don't have the money to medicate all of the children," she explains. "It would cost forty dollars to buy medicine." We tell her, through Svetlana, that we will buy the medicine for the children, and she begins furtively writing prescriptions and instructions to Svetlana.

Finally, we are led down a dark staircase and into a waiting room that will become our second home for the coming weeks. It contains a couple of hard chairs, a sink for washing our hands (required) and a door that leads into the room that is home to the toddler-aged children. Svetlana goes to the door of the room and has a conversation with one of the nurses, who goes into the back room. Svetlana smiles and tells us to ready our cameras. This is the satisfying part of the job for her as well—the part that makes all of the paperwork, court appearances, and logistics worthwhile.

She's prepared us to temper our expectations. Often, she explained, orphans have never seen a man before, as they are cared for each day by a staff made up of women. They also explain that the child may not immediately want to cuddle or show affection, as these bonds take time to form.

We wait. In a moment you will round that corner and we will be one step closer to being parents. I grab Kristin's hand and we look at each other and smile. This is one of those seminal moments in a marriage—we've been through the labor together, some of it at least, and now we'll enjoy the realization of you. She closes her eyes and I can tell we're both praying, silently, to ourselves, together. We're praying for a connection to you. We're praying that you'll like us now, and then grow to love us later.

You appear, first in Svetlana's arms. You're wearing a bright, garish, orphanage-sweater that has probably been worn by countless kids before you. Your hair is a little shaggy, but it's blond, curly, and beautiful. Your eyes are like big, brown almonds. You're not crying. You're just taking it all in.

Svetlana sits you on our laps, together. You're big and solid—I can feel it in you, even though there's never enough to eat in here. You stare at us with your big, brown eyes and I wonder if you're aware of the changes that will take place. We show you some books and a couple of toys. We say, "Mama" and "Dada" to you, while pointing at ourselves, eager to make the connection clear to you. You are very serious and quiet at the start, but then begin to smile and play. Your smile is beautiful—your cheeks are chubby and you even have a few little teeth. You throw a rubber ducky on the floor and say "dah!" in the most husky, yet teensyishly-endearing baby voice. We sit on the floor and roll a soccer ball back and forth before the nurses ask us to pick you up because they don't want you on the drafty floor. I'm glad they're looking out for you and your health.

And we try, in our own way, at the end of the night to assure you that we'll be back tomorrow. And the next day. And the next, until one day you can come with us.

I kiss you on the cheek and leave you at the end of the night, full of the assurance that God is good, and that you and your mother are the two most beautiful creatures I have ever seen.

◌ ◌ ◌

McDonald's is our promised dinner destination, and Sasha rolls his eyes when he is told where we're going. He seems like the type of guy who fries up a giant hunk of pork at the end of the night and washes it down with about a gallon of vodka or home brew.

McDonald's may be the bottom of the food chain in America, but here it is a shiny, gleaming mecca of cleanliness, familiarity, and comfort food. The brightest lights and best-looking people in Ukraine can be found under the Golden Arches. The land of the hamburger. The staff at the Simferopol McDonald's wears little company bandanas around their heads. They look like little Mc-Donald's bandits. Burger gangsters.

I want to roll out my sleeping bag and stay here. Right next to the birthday party going on behind the glass walls. Some little Aleksandr or Sasha is turning six, eating ice cream, and playing pin-the-tail-on-the-donkey, just like in the States.

◌ ◌ ◌

Finding forty bucks' worth of medicine in Simferopol is proving to be harder than anyone thought. We're armed with a handful of illegible (to us) prescriptions, a car, and a big driver (Sasha) who I'm still a little afraid of now but who I'll grow to appreciate and would like to have on my side if something ever goes down.

Sasha whips the Lada in and out of side streets and alleyways. It feels a little *Starsky and Hutch*-ish, really. We whip into a place. We go inside, Sasha yells at somebody in Russian, and I come out with a bottle of pills. The pill collection on the backseat is growing larger, and we finally ask Sasha to stop at the open-air market so that we can collect one last item.

The market is wild. Narrow footpaths lead through row upon row of kiosks (cigs, magazines) and open storefronts (shoes, sweatsuits) and actual stores (medicine, diapers, etc.). We walk by one vendor with every imaginable part one would need to build a Lada in a living room, if need be. Door panels, steering wheels, engine parts, axles, and everything in between.

Finally we buy the diapers and deliver them, with all of the medicine, to the orphanage where we are hugged and smiled at by the kind staff there. It's as useful as I've felt in a long, long time.

Dear Tristan,

We saw you again today, Son. Tristan Volodymyr Kluck. A strong name. Tristan means "son of thunder." Does that make me thunder? Does it matter? I love you so much. You smiled more tonight . . . I think you said "Dada." You ate a cracker and played the "book and ball" game with me where I give you the book, and then the ball, and then you give them back.

I can't stop looking at your picture on the digital camera. I feel silly, but I keep saying "lemme see Tristan." And then your mom and I pull out the camera (again) and flip through the pictures (again).

And we prayed for you tonight, Tristan. We prayed that our Lord would keep you safe from evil and prepare your little heart to be loved by us. We prayed that our bond would be stronger than the thirty days or sixty days we may have to wait to see you again. It's gonna be hard to be away from you, man. I miss you already.

Yours,

Dad

◻ ◻ ◻

For the rest of our stay in Simferopol we'll be bunking down with Milla and Sasha (yes, another Sasha). Milla is a doctor at the orphanage, and is one of the sweetest, most positive people I have ever met. She and Kristin took to each other instantly, despite the language barrier, and I would often see her squeezing Kristin's cheeks or kissing her in a grandmotherly sort of way. They would while away hours together puttering in the kitchen, with Kristin struggling through awkward phrases in Ukrainian or Russian, and Milla saying equally unintelligible but always complimentary things in response.

I feel sheepish for not looking forward to staying with a family. In the States my life seems to revolve around downtime—the times when I can get away and be alone, usually to read, watch sports, or play a video game. This tells my brain that it can shut down and I can just relax.

It takes Milla about ten minutes to completely win me over, however. She insists that we will not ever be eating a meal out in a café; rather we will take each meal at "Café Milla"! She's an amazing cook, and each night serves something that has a winning combination of noodles, potatoes, and sausage. Then it's tea and cookies for dessert. I could get used to this.

Our only complaint is that, in true European style, twin beds rule the night. After seven years of sleeping together, I feel like Ward Cleaver, leaving Kristin in her bed alone at night and padding across the room to mine. And insomnia is tough here, at someone else's place. There is nowhere to go, and nothing really to do with the sleeplessness. I'm worried because I haven't called my parents since we landed in Simferopol. The phone card didn't work or something. It's always something. Dial a bunch of numbers, listen to tones, wait, and then not have it work. The only reliable thing to do is visit one of these places where there's about fifty phone booths along the wall, you give the chick some cash, and then bada-bing, you're talking to Mom and Dad.

I sit out on the patio for a while, amidst the drying laundry, and look at the rest of the Soviet high-rises, stretched out for as far as the eye can see, thinking how strange it is to be sleeping in the home of a person who just a few years ago we would have called an enemy.

○ ○ ○

Dear Tristan,

Things I did today:

• I ate at McDonald's again. A Quarter Pounder with cheese meal, plus a Coke, for ten hrivnas (two bucks).

Hooray for culture!

• I bought a pipe in Yalta. This isn't going to be some C. S. Lewis "I'll buy a pipe and smoke it once" phase. I really do like the smell of pipe smoke.

• I went to the Black Sea. (How crazy is that sentence? Who the heck am I to get to go to the Black Sea?)

• I touched the armchair where our president, FDR, signed a treaty with Winston Churchill and Josef Stalin.

• I missed you today, and wished you were at the ocean with us.

Much Love,

Dad

Ukraine is a study in contrasts—from the cold, flat, gray urban sprawl of Kiev to the mountain switchbacks and coastal living in Yalta. It is those switchbacks, and the backseat of another small Lada, and gasoline fumes, that make me feel like I'm going to lose my breakfast (Snickers, Coke) on the road to Yalta.

Aside: they use real nudity on billboards along the highway here. I can't say that it isn't effective . . . I looked, and got busted.

Our first stop is a beautiful famous garden, with old trees, huge rose gardens, and tons of mums, dahlias, and calla lilies. The climate here is strange—almost Mediterranean—which is a nice reprieve from the Detroitish gray that hung over Simferopol.

We feel a little bit like high rollers here. First of all, we've still got a bunch of benjamins strapped to our waist, and stuff here is really, really cheap. Admission to the garden—five hrivnas (one buck). Sweet aforementioned pipe—about three bucks, American. And we're so grateful to everybody—Svetlana, drivers, Milla and Sasha—that we want to throw tips around like it's 1955 and we're Frank Sinatra. We stop at an American-style grocery and load up on junk—chips, pop, beer, Snickers, and a few nods to nutrition like bread, cheese, and soup mix—and walk out of there only about ten bucks lighter.

Next we're in the White Palace, which is the former home of the czars—most recently the last czar Nikolas and his family, who were all assassinated in the Revolution—and was the meeting site for FDR, Churchill, and Stalin at the Yalta Conference. Everything has been perfectly preserved since that meeting. Chairs still in the same place they were when the men met. We wear little cotton things over our shoes that go *swish*, *swish* as we glide over the hardwood floors. In each room there is an old lady standing and waiting who turns on the lights when you enter, and turns them off when you leave.

Our final stop, the Swallow's Nest, is a tiny stone castle built on a ledge hanging over the Black Sea. The castle has a tiny restaurant which I wish we could dine in tonight, like kings. The fresh sea air is cold and tangy, and far below us the waves crash against high cliff walls. I think, right now, we have the most interesting and exotic life in the world. My wife is Audrey Hepburn, and I'm James Dean. It's been a wild ride together.

◌ ◌ ◌

You're crying when they bring you into the little reception area tonight. I think it's the noise and commotion—plus the late hour. I begged the driver to take us over to see you after the Yalta trip. We couldn't stand the thought of letting a day go by without seeing you. There's another couple in the room—an Italian couple—

and their little boy is tearing around playing with a ball, relishing the attention. His name is Andrei and it looks like they've known him a little longer.

One of the nurses brings you a cracker and you calm down immediately. You clutch that little cracker in your chubby hand as though it's the last thing on earth, watching it all the while with your solemn brown eyes. You keep your eyes on us, when you're not eating. I'm more than a little obsessed with getting you to say "Mama" and "Dada"—probably to the point of being an annoyance to you. Though I just want you to know that we're going to take you home, God willing.

Life is good here, and going to visit you is beginning to feel like a comfortable routine. We know where to go and what to do, and the nurses are beginning to recognize us as your parents. They're trying hard here, and we appreciate that. It's cold in the rooms, but they bundle you up in a hodgepodge of warm, orphanage clothing.

Dear Tris,

I'm really enjoying your mother. That seems like a given, but I mean it, she's really special. We've spent the last six days together, basically in the same room, and it's been great. We've talked about God and life, and you most of all. How you almost say words, and how great you look in your hat.

She loves history and she loves seeing new things. We had a great time kicking around Yalta buying post-cards and stuff. She loves postcards. She's a silly girl. She stopped and played with some stray kitties outside

the apartment today, and I wish I'd had a camera to re-
cord that.

We're lucky to have her.
Yours,
Dad

○ ○ ○

I feel like I'm in rehab—America rehab. But instead of Tommy Lee being led into Hazelden with flashbulbs popping, it's me holed up in a little room with two beds and a dresser. No TV. No music. No video games. No phone. No friends. No work. No email. No editors.

I haven't thought about my writing career in a week, but I've written more in that week than I've written in a long time. America is a drag race, man. Who can get rich, or get tenure, the fastest. Ready, set, go. Bachelor's, master's, doctorate, backpack, goatee, cappuccino. Rinse. Repeat. Exhaustion. Svetlana seems like she's at the end of her rope. She seems like she's always on the verge of some kind of collapse. In America the middle-aged ladies call this fibromyalgia. It's all the rage. Everybody who's anybody in the States has fibro. It's the disease of the overworked, the underworked, the satisfied, the unsatisfied, the Christian, and the pagan. Its achiness and general malaise knows no borders. I think I'm getting it.

I went to the Internet café today for a little fantasy football fix. Peerless Price is questionable for this weekend (he'll be out of football by the time this book is published) with a pulled hammy. The Bears are considering benching Kordell Stewart (they should). The Colts have a bye this week. The Vikings are still undefeated.

Edgerrin James (he'll always be on my fantasy team) and Daunte Culpepper each broke the same small bone in their lower back this season. Makes you wonder. Injuries always come in groups.

The dogs here, called *pesicks*, all have a very distinct look about them. It's an unkempt, uncultured, sly look that says "Hey, I eat garbage . . . want to make something of it, tough guy?"

$\square$ $\square$ $\square$

There is a universality in watching sports, proven by the fact that I'm sitting here watching soccer with our host, Sasha. There's something cool and borderless about sports, drinks, and men.

"To Sasha and Milla," I say, raising my glass. Down the hatch. FC Moscow 1, FC Italia 0.

It's comforting and fun beyond belief to be sitting in a living room watching sports. This is something I would do back home—minus, of course, the soccer. Tris, nobody got girls in college like soccer players. They're willowy of frame, and have long hair, cool names (Jordan, Trevor), and parents with nice cars. Therein lies the appeal. They probably have Elvis Costello records too.

This also takes my mind off the fact that I'm convinced our driver is ripping us off blind. He's overcharging us every night, not that I know how to argue. I just feel mad because I wanted to like him, and he's been doing this ever since Svetlana left for Kiev on some other business. It cost thirty hrivnas a day with her around, and now, suddenly we're paying fifty and eighty hrivnas a day. The really frustrating part is that we have been generous and more than willing to pay him (and everyone) fairly.

It's raining in Moscow. "To Moscow" (glasses lifted). Down the hatch.

Russia just scored again and I exchange high fives with my host. This is fun. Not as fun as football at home with my dad, but still fun. These guys score goals so infrequently that they go absolutely nuts each time they score. This guy rips off his jersey. Just rips it right off, exposing his white flesh.

Yeah, I really don't appreciate getting ripped off by this gold-toothed thug. He rips me off again and I knock his gold teeth out and take them to the free market. He may have been a warhorse twenty years ago, but I wouldn't bet against me tonight.

◻ ◻ ◻

My Sweet Boy,

I saw you again today, Son. We didn't go outside today, like yesterday, but stayed in for three hours of solid play. You laughed a lot today. You were more expressive. You said "Dada." I thought about being angry at Crimea for making us leave soon, but it's hard to be angry when you're holding your baby in your arms and he's absolutely perfect. This, I learned today.

I sang the song "Take Me Back" from the Rocky soundtrack today, and you tried to sing the "do, do, do, do" part with me. Way cool man, way cool.

I'm still praying, buddy, that God will allow us to take you home this trip. But His timing is good, whatever it is.

I love you pal—thanks for a great night.

Dad

Today they bring out your little rocking horse and you're rocking like it's going to take you somewhere. You are committed to rocking, and are rocking hard. I love to rock. I miss my rocking chair here, and don't feel quite relaxed if I can't sit in the chair and listen to a couple of minutes of music each day.

You are a serious baby, intent on your purposes. Your mom wanted to pick you up off your horse to cuddle, but you would have none of it. You grasped the handles and the horse came up with you.

It's a beautiful day out today—about 65 degrees and sunny with beautiful fall colors on the trees—and the nurses finally come in to tell us to take you outside. The nurses are paranoid about cold drafts here (must be the years of living life with jankety windows) and bundle you underneath boots, a heavy coat, a hat with earflaps, and mittens.

You're drenched in sweat outside after about three minutes of play, and most of the garb comes off. It's weird, wanting to spend time with you, but doing it under their watchful eyes. We're eager to explore new things with you but scared of unwittingly doing something that would make them think we're bad parents. It's a gradual getting-to-know-you, under their observation and on their terms. And you're a true man of the soil. You're not satisfied just sitting in the dirt, but want to be rolling in it, digging in it, and, sometimes, eating it with your bare hands. All with us looking over our shoulders to make sure there isn't a nurse somewhere nearby. We'd been told here never to take a child outside without the proper clothing, because the grandmothers would appear from out of nowhere to read you the riot act and, sure enough, as if on cue an old lady gives us an earful because you're sweaty. There's no pleasing the babushkas.

The nurses kind of crabbily informed us that we needed to

get Tristan some shoes today. We're happy to get him shoes, and whatever else he needs, but we didn't know this was allowed or expected. So not knowing how the sizes work here, we traced his foot on a piece of paper and walked it to the open-air market which is about a mile or so down the road from the orphanage. We bought two pairs of little athletic shoes, a hat, and a jogging suit and returned to the orphanage, feeling a little proud of ourselves for venturing out on our own and coming back with a bagful of stuff.

"Too big," said the nurse, upon examining the shoes, which were probably nicer than anything he'd ever worn up to that point. Back we trudge, through the mud puddles, back to the open-air market to make a return, which, as you can imagine, is even more of a pain than making a return in the States.

Aside: the playground equipment here is all oddly militaristic—probably a holdover from communism. It's all little jeeps, boats, tanks, and rockets. Weird to think that perhaps this was how they trained orphan boys to be soldiers, years ago. Though I may very well be reading way too much into this.

You want to walk on your own so badly, but you still need practice. I hold on to a couple of fingers on each hand while you walk, determined. You laughed today, Son—the most delicious, throaty little chuckle we could have imagined. You like it when I lift you up high over my head, and I feel like we've turned a corner today. You are used to us now, and we're a part of your life. May the Lord protect you the time that we will have to be gone.

Yesterday we went to an Internet café and sent out a mass email announcing you to our friends and family. We were so excited to do it—to tell everyone about you—but part of me was scared to commit it to writing. We're afraid of losing you. We're afraid that somehow the thirty or sixty days will stretch into more and more months, or that somehow the court ruling would be "no." Or even that you would simply disappear. That we'll come back in a month with your book and ball, and simply be met with shrugs, head shakes, and blank looks—never to see you again. Or that your birth mother would suddenly come to her senses, or be in a position to care for you, and reappear to whisk you away, and we would have no recourse. We're essentially deaf, mute, and illiterate here. We're not charming. We're not cool. We speak in hackneyed little sentences with our own weird, contrived accents, things like "Want go to McDonald's" or "Please we see baby today."

It will be hard to love you with no reserve—no little inkling of self-preservation—until it is all legalized in the courts. Supposedly we're going to learn the court date soon, but that has yet to happen, and not being able to communicate with anyone about where the process stands is getting tiresome. We look forward to being your parents for more than just the few hours each day we're allowed. But our hope and trust is in the Lord, and we present these fears and worries to Him, hopeful that His goodness will overrule.

◌ ◌ ◌

In between visits to you we spend a lot of time walking around the streets of Simferopol, as our options are either to do this or to go back to the empty apartment with the scary security system (see: chapter 1). So we kick around the little shops and the market around the corner from our place. Kristin bought flowers from a few old ladies on the corner—zinnias and dahlias—and gave some money to a sad little girl, begging. It's hard to see that. Are we really helping, or just assuaging a guilty conscience? We'll never know.

> *Dear Tristan,*
>
> *The Ukraine is wearing on us both. We're tired of the watchful eye of the babushkas . . . they seem critical of everything we are trying to do for you, and we can't even argue with them in our native tongue.*
>
> *But your mom and I, we have each other. When she grabs my arm or I feel her hand on the small of my back in the crowded street, I know she's there. I know she's with me. That's romance. I pray that you will find the same thing someday.*
>
> *Dad*

I thank God for Milla and Sasha. Could two people possibly shower us with more kindness and hospitality? Tonight, Milla has prepared homemade chicken pot pie, which was delicious, not to mention labor-intensive for her. We try to make what conversation we can, and it's rewarding when both parties GET something. They just smile and push more food in front of us, and then thank US for eating with them. *Lord, pour out Your blessings on this house. Return a hundredfold their kindness, and let us know what we can do to express our gratitude.*

Because you're mine, I walk the line.

— Johnny Cash, *Walk the Line*

CHAPTER 3:
LIVING ON A PRAYER

This whole thing unfolds like the bad cliché it probably is. We get our hopes up that we might be able to take you home at the end of this trip. We have been praying and hoping to this end since the first day we met you in the orphanage.

And then this afternoon Svetlana comes into the apartment and tells us in her slightly cold, stoic, Eastern European way that we will be leaving. Tonight. And go ahead and get packed up now. No time to waste.

I get mad (not at her). I close the door and unleash a whole truckload of profanity not suitable for print here, directed at the governmental powers-that-be in Simferopol who were too prin-cipled to be bought, but who are sending us home without our son. I call down curses on their heads, and wish them all to be run over by the nearest Lada and then have their remains eaten by the nearest pack of hungry *pesicks*.

I can't pack. All I can do is cry. I look at the soccer ball, and your book, and I cry and hold Kristin. This is as bitter and hopeless as I've felt in a long time. All of the fears over leaving you—knowing that pneumonia is ripping through the orphanage, and knowing that the corrupt people in power here might just make you disappear—come back to haunt me now. And now we have to leave.

Svetlana is in rare form. Chimping around here, stressed out, as though every second counts (it does). For the first time in my life I don't care about being early, or even being on time. I start making demands, which I never do in real life (find my picture next to the word "compliant" in the dictionary). I ask that they take us to the orphanage to see Tris one more time.

I think about him waiting for our visit in the orphanage tomorrow, trying to get a feel for how the fourteen-month-old mind works. Will he feel openly betrayed? Will he worry about us? Kristin is a mess, too. We're both crying. We throw our dirty, greasy clothes into the suitcase and speed away. We stop at the orphanage long enough to give a book of pictures to a nurse and ask her to show them to Tristan. She acts like she's been through this before, and agrees to show him.

We rattle around the streets in the backseat of the Lada. Things were patched up with Sasha, the driver, but it will never be the same. He speeds us to the train station, where Svetlana tries, unsuccessfully, to buy us a berth to Kiev. She looks like she's going to explode. High-strung doesn't begin to describe her right now. Meanwhile, I feel empty. Ice man. Power Ted. Survival mode. Whatever they can throw at me can't be any worse than the news we just received.

From there it's more careening around the dark streets. It's raining here. It's always raining. A perfect night for this kind of news. Everybody's miserable. Finally we settle into a bus-station waiting room. And yes, Eastern European bus stations are every bit as scary as American Greyhound stations, filled with people who look like they just got paroled from prison. I look around the room, with everybody checking out the American hauling two big bags of nice stuff. I dare them with my eyes to try me.

My phone card miraculously works in one of the bus-station phone booths. I dial my parents and pour it all out to them. My mom prays for me on the phone, which never fails to make me choke up a little bit.

There's a strange little Shashlyk (shish kebob) hut next to the train station, where we get the first hot meal we've had all day. The hut is actually a canvas tent that sits over an open-wood oven. They stream American hip-hop music over the loudspeaker. Svetlana's calmed considerably since successfully buying us two one-way tickets (eighteen hours) to Kiev. We're going to see every nook and cranny of the Ukrainian countryside in great detail. It sounds like hell on wheels. The rain thumps down on the canvas, and I imagine myself boarding a bus without my son. This still hurts.

My Sweet Son,

Bad news always comes at night. Beware the late-night phone call. It's never good. I think mid-afternoon must be the safest time in the world. Nothing bad ever happens at 3 p.m.

They called Svetlana tonight and told her we have to

go to America and wait thirty days for you. Thirty days! I punched the wall. I paced the room like an animal. I looked at your diapers and your book and I cried angry tears. I can't leave you like this.

I miss you already. I'm sitting in a dank hellhole of a bus station. I was mad at God a while ago . . . I asked Him why He didn't fix it for us. Why He couldn't work out a miracle this time. Turn some water into wine and bring you home with us. But, alas, He chose not to. And we have to believe His timing is good, Son. He is good.

I'd like to stand on that judge's throat until he calls out your name, but I can't. So I will go home and pray for you. These are the labor pains. My eyes hurt from crying, and we'll both cry ourselves to sleep tonight.

But God is my strength and my shield. Vengeance belongs to the Lord. Hallowed be Thy name.

Just don't answer the phone at night.

Love,

Dad

◻ ◻ ◻

If God can be good on an eighteen-hour bus ride into Kiev, then He can be good anywhere. As are most bus rides, this one is kind of miserable—starting with the B-grade soft-porn flick that the driver decides to throw in about an hour into the trip. I've traveled with minor-league football teams my entire life, and successfully avoided the awkward "porno-on-the-bus" dilemma, but who knew it would take a trip to Europe to make it happen? I look over at Kristin and she just laughs. It's our first laugh since getting the news about Tris.

At this point there is nothing to do besides look out the window. We've long since ravaged our books, and have nothing to do but pray, talk to each other, and stare at the vast stretches of beautiful, untouched Ukrainian countryside. I've never been to the Great Plains states in America, but this is how I imagine it must have looked a century or so ago. Miles and miles of wide-openness. I see Ukrainian farmers driving horse-drawn carriages. It's like a bus trip through the late 1800s, made trippier by sleep deprivation and a diet consisting only of Snickers bars and Coke. There are stops at pit toilets to go to the bathroom—toilets that are just holes in the ground surrounded by crude brick walls. There are stops in the middle of the night at misty train stations, where people get off the bus and other people get on it. I can't believe I'm here. I feel like I'm living someone else's life.

The night lasts forever. Kristin takes two Tylenol PM tablets and is in a coma in a matter of minutes. I take two Tylenol PM tabs and am, besides (occasionally) the bus driver, the only person on the bus awake two hours later. I could never sleep on buses. If this were America, I would pad up to the little jumpseat behind the driver and chat him up for a while—I've done this on football trips and youth-group trips to Florida my entire life. There is a fat Ukrainian man sitting a few rows behind me with a giant walrus moustache. He looks like the golfer Craig Stadler, and his snores are like the throaty rumble of a Harley-Davidson engine. For more than a few minutes I consider walking back with my pillow and suffocating him.

○ ○ ○

Our arrival in Kiev is a blur. We're met by Lesya and Sergei again, and I'm glad to see them. They know we're disappointed, and I appreciate their care for us. We are whisked around the city in Sergei's car, on a frantic search for airline tickets. Finally, we find a Lufthansa agent who can get us on a flight out, tomorrow, for an exorbitant amount of cash which I unstrap from my belt and count out on the table. The posters in the office portray Lufthansa flights landing in warm, exotic locales. It's snowing outside. Kiev to Frankfurt to Detroit. We leave tomorrow.

We're deposited at yet another apartment, this one with a beautiful view of old-town Kiev. Out our flat's window I can see lights from the Kiev soccer stadium glowing in the distance, and can hear music and revelry from afar. There appears to be some sort of festival happening downtown. We shower (finally, thank You God, for hot water) and then set out for downtown.

We happen upon an underground mall, and after a long ride down an escalator, enter a mall that is American in appearance— bright lights, food court, and lots of pricey stores. We eat ice cream in a food court and for a moment feel like we're home. We spend the rest of the evening wandering the streets of Kiev, arm in arm, watching people and watching whatever festival they're celebrating happen in the streets around us. We stop on some steps and watch some skinny, cool-looking Ukrainian skateboard kids do tricks and then get run off by security. Finally dinner at McDonald's, a couple of chocolate croissants, and before we know it we're in the Kiev airport again.

◌ ◌ ◌

Strange Kiev airport situation: sitting in the lobby next to an

American guy with a ceramic gnome that looks like it's about to be gifted to someone. He's about my age, a pretty normal-looking guy from Omaha, Nebraska or Norman, Oklahoma. His name is Brett or Brent. Looks like the type of guy who drives a Camaro. He's in Kiev, he says, to pick up a girl he met online. "We really made a connection," he explains, trying hard to get us to believe that it wasn't a mail-order-bride situation. Either way, it's good to be talking to another American.

⌂ ⌂ ⌂

LATE NOVEMBER, TRIP #2

The thirty days went quickly, and now I'm back in the car, stressing out again, driving toward Detroit Metro Airport, which has come to feel like a second home. I am a human stress bomb. My wife fears that I'll be dead at thirty-five. Slow drivers. A wrong turn. Everything is bleak. It's only her and her good humor that gets me through. She validates without enabling (wow, how's that for psychobabble?), and usually has me laughing once I realize that everything will be okay.

What was unfamiliar and scary on the first trip, seems old hat now—the transatlantic flight, the connection in Germany, the Kiev airport (much less scary this time) and before we know it we're sleeping for twelve hours in a nice flat in Kiev (the one close to the town square with the sweet underground mall).

In Simferopol, Milla throws open the door and welcomes us back with open arms. It seems that she could hardly wait to start hugging and kissing us. Kristin is crocheting a scarf for her, as a token of our appreciation.

This trip will be fast, only a week, and will result, we hope, in our going to court to get official custody of Tristan.

> *Dear Tristan,*
>
> *Back in Simferopol. It feels like home this time—neither scary or dramatic. Just quiet. This is where I come to disappear. I am nobody in this city—just a husband and a father. I turn everything off here. No advertisements, no television, nothing applies to me. I am not a demographic.*
>
> *I tell Milla that our room feels like home and she kisses me three times on the left cheek. The room does feel like home. Four walls. Two beds. A mirror. A window. Not even the airplane was scary.*
>
> *In a half hour we'll see you, sweet boy.*
>
> *Love,*
>
> *Dad*

We're both excited and a little nervous to see you. Nervous that you would not know us, or would have changed a lot. When we enter the room you're seated in a little chair, with a towel wrapped around your neck, getting a haircut. You stare at us and stare at us. You're a little unsure of yourself after they hand you to us, but in a matter of minutes you're laughing, smiling, and playing as though we'd never left.

The big change is that you walked by yourself! We knew this change would come when we were gone, as you were so close before, but we so hated to miss your first steps. But now when we play "chase" you can walk on your own. There is no greater sound than your sweet, husky little baby laugh when you anticipate us pouncing on you and scooping you up. This is a joyful reunion and we thank God for it. We thank Him for bringing us through the thirty-day wait, and for helping us forget about it now. Now that you're in front of us.

The only bit of sadness was a story the nurses told, of you crying and waiting for us to come when the other children were being met by their adoptive parents. You knew, intuitively, what was happening, and it breaks our hearts to know you felt that way, even for a few minutes.

□ □ □

I get dressed this way for work almost every day. Shower. Shave. Shirt and tie. Suit pants. Suitcoat. Usually it is for a boring commute into a boring job at a boring desk. Today it is so that we can go to court, to vie for the right to be your parents.

It feels good to be dressed up here—and get out of the rugged jeans/boots/hat/coat wardrobe that we've been in every other day. We couldn't sleep last night—worried about the court date, no doubt—but we had a great time talking, laughing, and praying together.

Court is both very official and extremely rinky-dink. Like most Ukrainian buildings the courthouse suffers from an extreme lack of light. I count two light fixtures with bulbs, and three empty sockets. We're led into a concrete room with a very inviting rebar cage in one corner where, ostensibly, they put the very dangerous Ukrainian lawbreaking types. Thankfully, we get a wooden bench.

It's freezing. It's always freezing when I'm nervous, but I think it's also really freezing in here. I keep breathing into my hands, unable to warm them. The judge, a youngish woman, calls each of us to the stand to answer questions about why we want to adopt.

They're surprised, perplexed and unsure as to why a couple so young, who may be able to have biological children, would want to adopt. We pray that the Lord would give us the words to say, and shiver through our testimonies. We try to communicate that because we have so many blessings, we want to give blessings to someone who has none.

The judge leaves abruptly, and our translator, a very nice woman named Helena, informs us that they will be back soon with their decision. Decision? We thought this was just a formality, but it has felt a little bit too much like a very pivotal step in the process. We thought we would show up, smile, and sign some papers. This feels serious.

We're too scared to pray coherently so we just sit there, paralyzed, as the minutes tick by. I look at the rebar cage and feel something like sympathy for the men who have sat in it. I know now how they feel. Maybe we were too honest? Maybe our ideas were too radical? Maybe we should have told them that we tried, and failed, to have kids?

When she comes back with the decision, the yes, we both begin to cry and shake. Everyone congratulates us, and tells us that we are the real, official, parents now, but I won't feel safe until you're in our custody, and home safe with us. But for now, a legal document that calls us your mom and dad is way better than nothing.

My Sweet Son,

It's official, Son, as of this morning at about 10:00 a.m., you are ours! Tears of joy, my little friend, tears of joy.

The court scene was, as expected, very cold and in-

timidating. The courtroom itself was just a concrete cell with wood benches and a cage made out of rebar. Must be where they put the prisoners during real trials. Yikes.

We tried with all our might to communicate to the judge our love for YOU! I saw your little face the whole time, Tris. I prayed hard for you, man, and saw our pictures of you in my mind's eye. When they said yes I held your mother and cried tears of pure joy. I love you Tristan Volodymyr Kluck.

Dad

△ △ △

We go to McDonald's and eat a full celebratory meal, and then realize it is only 10:20 a.m. This morning felt like a lifetime.

We're all wrung out. After an afternoon nap, we take a walk through Simferopol and discover that everybody crosses the street underground in these cities, which is an unbelievably cool way to move people through a city. The tunnels are all lined with kiosks (smokes, magazines, toiletries, etc.) and we even find a little yarn shop where Kristin stocks up on crochet supplies.

We find a city zoo, and the admission is a whopping twenty cents, American. We go in and walk around to the displays of huge, bored-looking animals. We are almost all alone here, and it reminds me of the zoo scene in the first *Rocky*, where Rocky takes Adrian on a date. The intensity of the court date past, we feel like we can finally begin to enjoy the city. I stand for a long time and look at a lonely lion in a cage. He looks like a tired, old warrior, now bored with his life as a display-piece.

I wish Tristan was here.

○ ○ ○

This trip is over almost as quickly as it begins, and we are hard at work (or, I should say, Kristin is hard at work) on a thank-you note for the staff at the orphanage. We pore over our Russian/English dictionary, and the end result is, I'm sure, an embarrassing, but hopefully endearing attempt at a sincere thank-you. We add a big bouquet of salmon-colored gerber daisies to the note, along with a couple of boxes of chocolates.

The nurse at the orphanage turns and reads it aloud to the rest of the staff, and they seem genuinely touched. Our reality hits, though, that we won't be seeing you for another thirty days. As we walk you back toward your room to hand you off, your mom starts to cry. And then I start to cry. I've been crying a lot lately—probably more in the last two months than in my previous twenty-some years of life. I feel like Dick Vermeil, like I'm getting comfortable crying in public. Not entirely certain this is a good thing. We're crying through our broken hearts, and you're just trying to get to your little table, for lunch. I don't think the nurses know what to do with us. One sweet nurse, who knows a little English, keeps saying "Don't cry Mama e Papi."

○ ○ ○

I come very close to losing my mind in the Frankfurt Airport. I am operating under the apparently erroneous assumption that just because we have a ticket that says "Frankfurt to Detroit" that we will actually be traveling on that flight to Detroit. The German lady at the desk, in very lovely English, explains that they've overbooked the flight and there is a "good chance" we'll have to spend the night in Frankfurt. "Thanks so much, keep us posted," I reply, smiling. I then turn to Kristin who can tell by the look in my eye that I'm going to lose it.

One advantage of modern airline travel is that now because of the miracle of computerized monitors throughout the gate area, you can actually watch your overbooked flight and give names to the faces who will be boarding ahead of you and thus ruining your trip. I watch my own name, Kluck, T, on the screen, hoping that my "Wait List" status will turn to "I'm finally getting the heck out of Europe and going home tonight" status. Understand that I have nothing against Europe, or travel, I'm just more than ready to be home. So much so that spending a night in a beautiful European city (Frankfurt) is enough to send me into a blind rage, which, of course, I don't share with the ticket lady. I look at her and smile, occasionally, just to let her know we're still waiting and that I still have the utmost faith in her ability to get us home.

Kluck, T, isn't making much progress up the list. The name looks German because it is. It used to be Von Kluck. I come from a long line of short-tempered Germans who would all be livid by now if they were here in my place. The real Kluck, T, is having blood pressure issues and has decided that he *will* be boarding the flight.

○ ○ ○

Cut to Newark, New Jersey, and another flight delay. We got on the flight in Frankfurt, with about thirty seconds remaining until they raised the landing gear and took off. Who cares. We were on the flight and going home! However, we are now faced with the unfortunate reality of Newark Airport. It's the middle of the night here, and we're surrounded by other weary, cynical travelers. It's Thanksgiving weekend. Big deal. Our plane can't take off because of a nice winter storm outside. We've been awake for twenty-four hours. Tired of the general public—they all look like the enemy at this point. Travel is like a game. It's like reality television. Beating the game means getting home.

There are three loud, obnoxious girls working the Delta desk at our gate. They're talking about boys, about dates, and about how they "can't wait to get out of there." Tell me about it. Finally, by 10 p.m. we dash through the freezing rain to board a puddle jumper which after a wobbly takeoff, a bumpy flight, and a death-defying landing, puts us in Detroit by midnight. I never thought I'd be happy to see Detroit.

I waited patiently for the Lord; he turned to me and heard my cry. He lifted me out of the slimy pit, out of the mud and mire; he set my feet on a rock and gave me a firm place to stand. He put a new song in my mouth, a hymn of praise to our God. Many will see and fear and put their trust in the Lord.

—*Psalm 40: 1–3*

CHAPTER 4:
WHEN I SEE YOU SMILE

It takes us about a week, once we get home, to discover that there are no remaining tickets anywhere in the world that will get us to anywhere in Europe before January 3. Crushing disappointment. We're as low as we've been, since this thing started, feeling like officially we have a son sitting in an orphanage in Ukraine, and there's no way to physically get to him. This is a bitter pill. My wife is swearing a lot more now. This is what bitterness feels like.

So we spend a forgettable Christmas without Tristan and decide to buy tickets to go from January 3–11. No problem. We've waited over a year to get Tristan, what's a couple of extra weeks. And then, today, we get a call from our Bethany rep informing us that the president of Ukraine has declared January 1–8 a "national holiday." The president, in his infinite wisdom, has decided to "shut the country down," meaning a nice, long break for everyone that promises to be a nice morale booster for Ukrainians everywhere, but completely messes up our plans to bring Tris home. Ukrainian government offices aren't exactly snappy and efficient when operating at full strength (think inner-city Department of Motor Vehicles, only slower) so now we find out they won't be operating at all.

Meanwhile, the dollar signs are adding up—seven hundred bucks for a ticket change, another $500 in "extra expenses" from the third trip, and $350 for another Ukraine visa. At this point we're looking at massive debt either way. To add insult to injury, we purchased a car from a friend (a used Volvo wagon; I thought I was going to be "used Volvo wagon guy"—big mistake) that promptly needed $1,200 worth of work just to make the engine turn over.

Bethany assures us that this is "nobody's fault." Kristin chews out the Bethany rep on the phone and then calls back a few minutes later to apologize. They understand. They've never seen an adoption go this badly.

Our faith is taking a beating. We're answering a lot of questions from people who "want to know how to pray," but feel like we're just telling the same sad story over and over again. We feel like we'll never see our son. We set out, idealistically, to change the system and shed positive light on international adoption, and now we can't even bring *one* kid home, much less account for the others. However, the complete awfulness of our situation has no doubt turned off countless other couples who may have been interested in international adoption. It's hard to say we're trusting God, much less to actually trust Him.

The low point comes at a church potluck, when the pastor thanks God for "making things happen in His perfect timing." Kristin is in tears. We're not sure about God's timing right now. Later, a guy asks me to stand up and share a little bit about the adoption. I start talking about Tris, and the process, and soon *I* am in tears. We are prayed for by the group, and this never ceases to impact me, emotionally. I remember crying as a child when my mother would read Scripture and pray for me. It's a powerful thing.

◠ ◠ ◠

A week later a friend from our neighborhood, who is a deacon from our church, brings a check for $2,000 by our house, from the church diaconate fund. We are ashamed of our doubts, and thankful, and are reminded of the ways the Lord has been faithful to us through this process. Like the Israelites in the desert, we are reminded of our shortsightedness.

◠ ◠ ◠

January 10 and we are in Detroit again, this time in the ultra-swank Westin Hotel, which is attached to the new terminal at Detroit Metro. We have an early-morning flight tomorrow, and opted to spend our last American night without children in a hotel here on the premises, partly to celebrate, and partly to avoid any early-morning "getting to the airport" issues. The room is unbelievable. Sleek and modern. Lots of stainless steel and pale wood. Cushy carpet. I'm typing this in a robe that I am very tempted to steal.

The shower is especially meaningful, as it will probably be the last one we have for three days or so. From here it's on to New York (LaGuardia), and then across town to JFK, an overnight flight to Prague (what a great city), to Kiev, and finally an overnight train to Simferopol. Everything will be new to Tristan. He's spent his entire life confined in the orphanage, save for a few outside walks we took on the grounds. We've been praying about logistics—like what he'll sleep in in the flats and hotels we stay in until we get back to the States.

◻ ◻ ◻

Upon arrival in Kiev, we get the good bit of news from Lesya that there are two plane tickets available to Simferopol, which gives us a chance to get a hot meal in Kiev before catching the plane. We're met there by a very enthusiastic Svetlana, who is jumping up and down and waving when we land. She's so very nice. We've been through a lot together. This whole thing is beginning to take on that "last day of summer camp" feel, where we realize we'll be saying good-bye forever to people with whom we've been through a lot.

Svetlana takes us to the market, where we load up on fruit, candy, and pop for the orphanage workers and the other kids. We're also hoping to leave $300 for the doctor at the orphanage to purchase another round of medicine. There aren't many times in life I can point to in which I felt truly useful, but these are among those times. It's amazing what three hundred bucks can do over here.

The scene at the orphanage is a little anticlimactic (in a good way). We're there for all of about thirty minutes. It's simple. So much so that we wonder why we couldn't have just driven off with him at some point during our first trip. We're there long enough to change Tristan's clothes, give the money to the director, and share our treats with the nurses. Most of the kids are down for an afternoon nap.

Even having Tristan in the car with us is a mind-blow, realizing he's never been off the premises. A note about the car: nobody uses car seats here. The child sits on your lap in the backseat, and you hope your driver is feeling alert and safe. Yikes. There has to be a happy medium between America, where the child seemingly has to be in a car seat until he's eighteen, and this.

We drive quickly to an office where Tristan has a passport photo taken (note: this is really cute), and then back to the apartment to pack quickly. They're holding the plane for us when we get to the airport. The babushkas have swaddled Tristan within an inch of his life, and soon, on the plane, he's sweating buckets. The poor guy is overheating, but we can't remove an inch of clothing without drawing the ire of the old ladies on the plane. Otherwise, the flight goes unbelievably well. He plays and sits on our laps and has a great time.

In Kiev we're taken to another nice apartment—well stocked with towels and American stuff (movies!)—but completely in the middle of nowhere. There's not even a kiosk around to buy our daily ration of pop and Snickers. We'll chill here for a couple of days and then process out at the American embassy in Kiev, and then take an eleven-hour car ride to Warsaw, where we'll do more "processing out."

Tristan is amazing. He's running through the apartment and seems to have a nonstop motor for "play." If he's missing the orphanage at all, it's not showing. Dinner is another adventure. We make a pot of gross soup from a mix (it's all we have) and Tris eats . . . and eats . . . and eats. We say things like "look at him eating, he was so hungry" and "it's so cute."

Cut to the middle of the night. We've pushed two cushy arm-chairs together and made a makeshift "bed" for him. At about

2 a.m. we hear a variety of strange gastronomical noises coming from his vicinity. "It's nothing . . . probably normal," we both say, exhausted, before enjoying our first night of bed-sleep in a long time.

There's no delicate way to say what we find in the morning. He's covered in poop almost head to toe. Yikes. Scramble. We draw a bath for him and he hates it. Screaming and squirming. We realize that bath time must not have been a fun experience in the orphanage.

The days kind of crawl by, but not in an unpleasant way. We're enjoying being parents, and I think he's enjoying being our son. We venture out into the calf-deep snow and take a walk with Tris, in search of a kiosk and some pop. These walks constitute our "big outings" for the day.

The night before we are to "process out" to Poland, the stomach flu hits our family with a vengeance. Kristin starts in the wee hours of the morning, and by the time Lesya and her husband arrive in his BMW to drive us to the embassy, I am hung over the toilet. "Can we do this tomorrow?" I ask. The look in her eyes tells me, emphatically, that I will be dragging myself to the embassy—today—and sooner rather than later. You don't argue with a Ukrainian woman who has a cellphone around her neck. I've heard her reaming people out before, and I don't want to be the guy getting the reaming.

In the car I focus on taking deep breaths. In and out. By this time, Kristin is still feeling awful but seems to be on the mend a little bit. I gaze out the front window and try to keep my cookies down, so to speak. The traffic is heavy. Stop and go. It seems hot in the car.

It happens so fast, that nobody really seems to notice the fact that I've lost my breakfast all over the front of Lesya's car. This is a low point in life. I start apologizing profusely. Then I start cleaning up. Just for good measure, I yack again on the steps of the embassy. There is probably some deeper symbolism here, though it escapes me at the moment.

Mercifully, there are some toys in the American embassy which, inside, magically looks just like an American government building where kids get a sucker, and Mom and Dad get to wait in line for a really long time. Actually it isn't too bad, and soon we're back at the airplane-themed café, where we'll take alternating trips to the bathroom, while trying to corral an eighteen-month-old who, like the Mentos commercial, is fresh and full of life. He just wants to walk, while his mother and I just want to curl up in the fetal position and die. I keep a running prayer going almost the entire time . . . praying for the Lord to either help us get through this, or for Him to take me (just kidding—sort of).

After what seems like forever, the driver arrives to drive us through the night to Warsaw, Poland. Though I am on death's doorstep, I still feel good enough to realize that our driver looks just like Patrick Swayze, circa *Roadhouse*. He's got the mullet and everything. Though I can't say that I relish the thought of eleven hours in his car. Thankfully—and this is another answer to prayer—Svetlana appears with a syringe full of medicine. And right there, in the middle of the sidewalk and with no argument from me, she injects a needle full of whatever into my bum. I say "whatever" because to this day I still have no idea what was in there, except that in an hour or so I felt markedly better.

The trip is an answer to prayer on many levels. For one, I now know what it feels like to pray "without ceasing" and see those prayers answered. Tristan is an angel. He sits on his mom's lap and sleeps for the majority of the eleven-hour journey. My only interaction with Swayze is at the Polish border where he requests a fistful of cash so that he can bribe the guards and move us to the front of the line. Fine. Done. I probably would have sold my own body at that point, to get to a clean room and a warm bed.

We arrive in Warsaw at about 4 a.m. and it is oddly empty and serene. Lots of tall buildings, lights, and empty streets. Warsaw is big and modern in a way that Ukraine, even Kiev, isn't. It feels almost American, and around the corner from our little hotel (very nice, comfortable) there is a McDonald's and a Pizza Hut (thank You, Lord). The room is wonderful. It's the first dwelling we've been in that doesn't feel "Eastern European" (read: the furniture is comfortable and the lights work). There is even a crib in the room for Tris, and by morning he has rocked the crib out into the middle of the room so that he can get a better look at us. We awake to find him staring at us with his big, almond eyes. He's a beautiful kid. Wow. And he's ours.

We spend several days in Warsaw just "getting healthy." And for us, getting healthy means lots of meals at McDonald's and Pizza Hut. We also find some time between meals to get out with a guide and see some of the cool historical sections of Warsaw, of which there are many. This is one of those rare times in life when "outside" responsibilities are minimal—there are really no set obligations for us here, other than to enjoy ourselves and get Tristan's American visa—until our flight leaves in a couple of days.

We use the time to get accustomed to being a family of three, instead of just two young lovers on an adventure. It occurs to us during this interval that we've aged considerably, but also that we've been richly blessed by the little Ukrainian in the crib.

PART 2

Dima

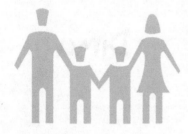

There are three things that men can do with women:

Love them, suffer for them, or turn them into literature.

—Neil Young

CHAPTER 1:
HIT WITH A FEW SHELLS, BUT I DON'T WALK WITH A LIMP: INFERTILITY

2004–2008, Michigan

An introductory paragraph to this section: this was written during a painful time in our life. Things were difficult in our church. Our response, in retrospect, wasn't always the godly response. The things that were said, and done, we knew then and know now were not intended to cause us pain. We made a lot of hard things even harder due to our attitudes and responses to people and we apologize both to our church as a body, and to those people individually. But we've left most of this as is, mainly in the name of "authenticity" and to help people who are going through similar struggles alone to feel not so alone.

○ ○ ○

The church lobby has become a gauntlet, of sorts. How do I get Kristin, who just started her period (the official physiological signal that—for another month—our "Not Pregnant" status hasn't changed), past the well-intentioned but superenthusiastic ladies in the corner who are jumping up and down with glee— thrilled at the news of another young couple expecting another baby? How will she respond to the friend who pulls her aside and, in hushed tones, tells her about her pregnancy, and about how she "didn't want [her] to hear from anyone else"? Will she break down in tears (which would be okay)? Or will she just turn in another Oscar-worthy performance, letting the friend know that she is thrilled for her, and so glad she told her in person— only to come home and *then* break down in tears (also okay)?

How will she respond to the infant baptism on the program today—you know, the one in which Big Family invites grandparents, brothers, sisters, cousins, aunts, and uncles onto the podium to celebrate Big Family growing one child bigger? Scripture is read. The baby is sprinkled. The baby cries, cutely—more of a coo, but not too much. Big Family explains why they named child after Biblical Figure. As members of the church we are asked to stand and pledge that we will agree to somehow help raise this child, who is somehow now in the covenant family (but not yet justified), in the way that it should go. We stand up. We mouth the words and mean them, sort of. We stare straight ahead. Rinse and repeat eleven months later when Big Family cranks out another child. And we truly believe that we will help raise the child inasmuch as (despite the cynicism here) these people are our friends and brothers/sisters in Christ and, if we stay at URC, we'll most likely be spending a lot of time together.

All the while we glance occasionally at our five-year-old, sitting and coloring, who we love more than anything except, I suppose, God. He's beautiful. He's enough. He is, for the most part, blissfully unaware of the pain that Mom (and sometimes Dad) feels every thirty or so days, and some days in between. Going through the adoption, I remember dreaming about this moment—coming to church with Tristan, having him sitting with us, singing the songs. Thinking about that, and how badly I wanted it and how God gave him to us, almost makes me cry. Tears of joy to match the tears of this new, ongoing pain.

Studies show that women have associated the pain of infertility with the pain of losing a loved one. After going through this with my wife, I can see why. There is a constant and sometimes unpredictable grieving process for her. The grieving process for men is different, as I think it often has more to do with keeping our wives' heads above water. When we hear a friend encourage his younger brother to "just get married and make babies," as if one just "makes babies" on command, it hits me because as someone who writes about sports, I'm around unintentional fertility all the time. The number of total illegitimate children sired by my interview subjects in *Facing Tyson* hovers around a hundred and is still growing. No exaggeration. And while I was taught well by my parents that life isn't fair, this still hurts. A lot.

We know the statistics—that one in four couples struggle with infertility at some point. Still, we feel profoundly alone. We're grieving and are still required to "laugh with those who laugh." We are all but told to "be happy for your friends, it will make you feel better" which we do, not because it makes us feel better but in order to keep the friends that we haven't managed to alienate through our weirdness about this.

I wish, at times, we could put out a church-wide press release saying something to the effect of: "For Immediate Release: Hey, this is really hard for us and while, on paper, we're happy for you and your pregnancy, it's difficult for us to hug, get excited, or come to your baby shower. Please accept this nice diaper bag and know that we care."[1]

Social convention, or perhaps cowardice, keeps us from sending such a release but part of me thinks it would still be helpful. Not so much as a hedge against future situations; just so that people know we care about them, but that for a while we'll need to care from afar. And so that they will continue to be our friends, and act normal, but understand when we don't hold their babies, and sometimes have to leave the room when the childbirth/labor stories start. It's not that we don't share in their joy; it's just that we can't share in their joy right then, in that way. Sort of like not talking about how awesome your career is, around your buddy who's been unemployed for a year and a half.

◠ ◠ ◠

Not getting pregnant immediately isn't a huge deal in the beginning. For the first year, you say things to each other like "It often takes couples a year or so to get pregnant once they start trying." You still feel genuinely thrilled for your friends' pregnancies, and are happy to be around babies because you'll be having one yourself. You do the mental math, and realize that if you get pregnant within a couple of months, you and Pregnant Friend will be Pregnant Friends together and that will be awesome. Your kids will go to school together (okay, homeschool in the case of most of our church families), and then one day they'll grow up and we can arrange their marriages.

Gradually that feeling goes away, as Pregnant Friend carries her baby to term and then delivers. There are some ups and downs in between. You're late for your period one month—and I write this as though it is also my period, because in a way it is now. You're so late you go to the drugstore and buy some pregnancy tests. You hold off on taking the test right away, preferring instead to hold on to the euphoric feeling that this might be the month. You go to your small group Bible study, which is crawling with ladies who are either pregnant or nursing, and for the first time you don't want to punch all of them in the face for talking about nothing but babies or how long their labor was. It's actually okay, because you might be one of them soon.

The next morning you rip open the package and go on the stick. All the while, of course, you're praying together that God will prepare your hearts for whatever happens, good or bad. You haven't told any of your friends yet that you're struggling with infertility, because this could be the month. And besides, when, and how do you make something like that public? And there it is, on the stick, larger than life: Negative. Not pregnant. On some sticks you can't help but read the messages like "Don't you feel silly for hoping now?" and "If you'd just waited another day or two you would have started your period."

You go to the sofa where you cry together with your spouse. This is also where you would've gone to celebrate together, which is a weird juxtaposition. You hold her, and she cries, and you try to pray but can't. You cried here last month too. Sometimes it's hard to pray anything besides asking God why He would put you through a tease like that.

□ □ □

By the end of the second year of infertility, you've become comfortable writing the words "sperm count" on paperwork, and going to various doctors to discuss various options. These visits are differing degrees of awkward. You wonder about the tenuous link between "faith" and "just trusting" and doctors trying to explain how they make babies in laboratories and then freeze the rest of the embryos. You get a sample collection cup to take home (yeah, it's for collecting *that* sample) that the hospital has gone to great pains to make look like a cup you might use in the cafeteria to get a fountain Diet Coke. You walk self-consciously through the lobby hoping with every fiber of your being that you don't run into someone you know there. You do, of course. It's a young girl in your church who is studying to be a doctor. Cue nervous tic and uncontrollable sweating. You make small talk, and hope she doesn't notice.

You sit in a tiny doctor's office with your wife and two young interns, as the fleshy doctor behind the desk lays out various options. He's the Midwest's Foremost Authority on something. His glasses don't fit right and he's sweating a little bit, which gives him the look of an insane person. Or a college professor. You hear him tell you that "I can make you pregnant, and many couples have sat where you're sitting." It's nice, you think, that he's so good at making babies. Creating life. Nice that God has this guy to fall back on, apparently. When you're not fidgeting with a paper clip, you squeeze your wife's hand. You know already that it's the two of you against the world. This guy has no idea that he's not The Creator. (Remember, all this is happening *after* the "it will never happen" diagnosis.) He doesn't understand your point of view and the fact that your faith—which is in shreds but is still a faith—may not allow you to do what he's suggesting. How much of this science is "common grace" and how much of it is playing God? We don't know the answer, because until now, we never thought we'd have to think about it. And what happens to the embryos, made with our genetic stuff, that aren't needed? Thinking about that makes my head spin. The room gets hot and now I'm sweating buckets like the crazy doc. The primary problem isn't just money, for us it's ethics too, but if it was, common grace is still looking pretty expensive. "The treatments are $12,000 per round," Crazy Sweaty Doc explains. "And it's no guarantee that they'll take right away."

What the doctor doesn't understand is that writing is neither lucrative, nor does it provide health insurance (which you're currently wildly overpaying for in one of the great injustices of American life). There's no way your feeble insurance will cover this procedure and what remained of your savings has been "lived on" in pursuit of a writing career that may never happen. You realized recently that professional writers often have a rich parent or uncle who can bankroll them during the lean years. You have no such relative. But it's too late. You're addicted and, you feel, called.

On the way out you're informed that your insurance won't cover the office visit. That will be $150. Help yourself to a mint on the way out and make sure you fight back the tears until you get to your car.

◻ ◻ ◻

In spite of the heavy darkness, God is blessing us richly during the second and third years of our infertility. It has been easy to feel like the only way that God could possibly be faithful, in this, would be to give us a pregnancy; however, in His sovereignty, He has been faithful in so many other ways.

We have, for the first time in our life, realized the depth of support inherent in the body of Christ. It was hard to tell our friends, but my wife crying through all of her Bible studies kind of gave it away anyway. We prayed with the elders of our church, when we all gathered on some bad pleather sofas in the church's tiny library. We both cried with them, they read Scripture, and they prayed both that we would get pregnant and that we would be able to recognize God's sovereignty in the midst of the pain, and in the event that we never conceive.

It's as good as we've felt in a long time. We feel something akin to what Hannah must have felt after she confided in Eli, the bumbling priest, in 1 Samuel. Hannah got her baby eventually. All the girls in the Bible got their babies, eventually. But we got the feeling that Hannah might still have been okay if she didn't, because Eli heard her, and he understood.

Our friends are bearing our burdens in other ways. They've become mindful of our struggle, and try hard to make any gathering including women not all about the baby, but even still, we don't want to feel like the wet blanket.

They send Scripture. We open our mailbox during the week and find a handwritten card with a verse mailed to us each day for a month. We appreciate this more than we will ever be able to communicate, because what our friends don't realize is that we haven't opened our Bible in a month.

I'm blown away by my wife's character because time and again she makes wonderful shower gifts and is genuine in her joy with these women, who are among our closest friends on earth. They know how hard it is, and have, I know, prayed with and for us.

I have pulled the occasional all-nighter with God, fasting and praying after my wife has cried herself to sleep. I open up my Bible and lie on the floor, pleading with God to have mercy on my wife. I feel like I've gone beyond merely asking for a baby, and have begun to ask for wisdom, and realize that, maybe for the first time, I'm relying on Him to really sustain us, instead of relying on my salary, my benefits package, or our fertility specialist.

God has also given us His Word—specifically Hannah's story in 1 Samuel. It is encouraging not because Hannah gets her baby (Samuel) at the end of chapter 1. Rather, it is an encouragement because Hannah dealt with a woman (Peninnah) who "kept provoking her in order to irritate her" (v. 6). It is an encouragement because Hannah also struggled "year after year" (v. 7). Hannah wasn't like the "friend" in so many well-meaning infertility stories who either tried a new procedure and got pregnant, or, "just gave it over to the Lord" and then God "blessed" her with a child. Hannah is an encouragement because she is the friend who has struggled for a long time, and because there is nobody at church who can quite understand what you're going through. The text goes on to explain that "whenever Hannah went up to the house of the Lord, her rival provoked her till she wept and would not eat" (v. 7). The Sabbath was anything but a day of rest for Hannah, and there were probably weeks where she felt like she couldn't do it.

And we learn that Hannah also dealt with a husband, Elkanah, who meant well, but who occasionally said famously stupid things, like in verse 8 when he asked, "Don't I mean more to you than ten sons?" It's the kind of thing, as a husband, you think in desperation. You probably even say it. You want to mean more than ten sons, but you can't. It goes deeper than that. It's different than that.

Hannah also experienced "bitterness of soul" (v. 10). We have been assured that it's okay to grieve, but that feeling bitter, ripped off, screwed over, or cheated is out of bounds. This is the special burden that Reformed thinkers carry. We can't blame spiritual warfare, or a demon, or the devil lurking around the corner. We believe that God is sovereign in all things, and He has placed this in our lives to sanctify us. So why would He choose to sanctify us in this way? Especially when no one else in our church seems to have been "blessed" with this special form of sanctification. We're told to "let go and let God," but not being granted the desire of your heart, something you've been told since little girlhood is good and right, is bound to produce some bitterness. There is comfort though, in knowing that Hannah felt the same way. However, in the midst of that pain, she still "wept much and prayed."

So much so, that she looked drunk. "As she kept on praying to the Lord, Eli observed her mouth. Hannah was praying in her heart, and her lips were moving but her voice was not heard. Eli thought she was drunk and said to her 'How long will you keep on getting drunk? Get rid of your wine'" (vv. 12–14).

So Hannah, after having to deal with her well-intentioned but nonetheless insensitive husband (I've been this character) then encounters a priest with a less-than-dazzling track record and a penchant for putting his foot in his mouth. But rather than lash out at Eli, as we have been tempted to do with the Elis in our situation, Hannah corrects him, and proceeds to pour out her soul to Eli in the Lord:

"Not so my lord," Hannah replied, "I am a woman who is deeply troubled. I have not been drinking wine or beer; I was pouring out my soul to the Lord. Do not take your servant for a wicked woman; I have been praying here out of my great anguish and grief." Eli answered: 'Go in peace, and may the God of Israel grant you what you have asked of him'" (vv. 15–17).

Verse 18 explains that Hannah "went her way and ate something, and her face was no longer downcast."

God's faithfulness began, for Hannah, before she became pregnant with Samuel, and we have seen similar blessings in our life. In the darkest moments, it seemed like there would never be anything but "the issue." But God blessed us with distractions, good times with friends and family, great meals, and, most of all, our son Tristan.

◻ ◻ ◻

While obsessing about pregnancy, it has been easy for us to forget how much we loved adopting Tristan. He's getting old enough now to ask us to tell him the story about how we "came and got him at the orphanage." It's a fun story to recount—we tell him about the long bus rides, the rickety old airplane we took from Kiev to Simferopol and back again ("What's rickety? Was it silver? Did it have cracks in it?"). The pictures come out. We see ourselves standing, with Tris, in front of the orphanage on a chilly fall day. Pictures of me teaching him to walk, pictures of him eating a cookie. Pictures of Kristin feeding him his first bowl of soup, and then giving him his first bath. Pictures of Kiev looking huge, gray, and mysterious. The golden domes juxtaposed with the Soviet high-rises that looked like parking garages, but that we called home during our weeks there. We see Lesya, our interpreter. We remember the frantic calls to Dr. Dubrovsky, whom we never met, but who provided much peace of mind throughout the process.

In struggling with infertility, we never lost our desire to adopt again, and looking at the pictures with Tris has reminded us how faithful God was during those weeks in Ukraine. Adoption never seemed like a "fallback" to us—in fact we adopted the first time not knowing that we would be unable to have biological kids. And it doesn't seem so now, even though the infertility looks dark and final. The adoption, much like our first, is an object of great excitement, if not great challenges. What starts as an idea gains steam as websites are searched and information is gathered. The adoption process is daunting—it's an endless maze of paperwork, phone numbers, mailings, and finally, travel—and it's easy to be jealous of couples who can just get pregnant and have a baby nine months later. The first step is a meeting with our caseworker and a perusal of each country's requirements.

We are perhaps broker (a word?) than we've ever been in eleven years of marriage. We learn that there isn't much of a precedent for struggling entrepreneurs adopting. Many adoptive parents are older and more established, or have the kind of secure "big company" job that will allow them the time and money to adopt. That was us, the first time around.

Our adoption caseworker, Jennifer, is wise beyond her years. She "deals" with us, the infertile couple, by sharing in our excitement for adoption, answering our many questions, and not act-ing like we're insane for wanting to adopt again when we barely have enough money coming in to pay next month's bills. She's the opposite of emotional, but she's also the opposite of cold, if that makes sense. She is what God knew we needed.

And we begin, again, to look at maps, and pray. Looking at maps is one of the things we love doing together. The city names— Donetsk, Sevastopol, Odessa, Vinnitsia—all seem big, exotic, and cool again. We watch *Everything Is Illuminated* because it takes place in Ukraine, and we see some of the places we saw when we adopted Tris. We can imagine ourselves there again, buying candy at kiosks, watching the men look tough and the girls smoke cigarettes, and being driven around in the backseats of Moskvich cars that have been around since communism was in its heyday.

And we can imagine being led into the orphanage, walking down the dark hallway for the first time. It smells like public school. It smells like cold and dark. And we remember what it was like to round the corner and see Tristan Volodymyr Kluck for the first time.

NOTE

1. We really do care.

This is Sanchez. He's a notary public.

— Royal Tenenbaum, in *The Royal Tenenbaums*

CHAPTER 2:
NEEDLE IN THE HAY: A FALSE ALARM, A FISTFIGHT, AND A CHURCH MEETING

Kristin looks frantic when she enters my office. She's in that heavy-breathing/crying/clutching the phone state which either means that somebody is dead or we have just come into a lot of money. Considering my earning power of late, I anticipate the former.

"We've got a little crisis," she says. "But a good crisis."

She sits and explains that she just got off the phone with Jennifer The Social Worker, from Bethany Christian Services. It'd been a long time since we'd heard from Jennifer. We had filed paperwork months ago, qualified for a loan, and been told that we'd have to wait until 2009 to adopt again.

"There's a little girl in Ukraine," Kristin explains. "Another adoptive couple saw her in the orphanage and called Dr. Dubrovsky. He then called Jennifer and said 'I have a baby for the Klucks.'"

I get a chill and, for the first time, pivot my desk chair completely away from my computer. I motion for Kristin to come and sit on my lap. This is intriguing news indeed.

◻ ◻ ◻

I wish we had our own notary public, like Sanchez, in the movie *The Royal Tenenbaums*, who stepped out of a bus with Royal and immediately started notarizing. Our life, the past two weeks, has been an endless stream of paperwork, notarizing, and apostiling.[1] I don't know what people do who don't know notary publics. Our go-to notary, Becky, who also conveniently works at our doctor's office, was unavailable this time, so we've been on a citywide search for friends, or friends of friends, who can help us jump through this very important adoption paperwork hoop.

Regarding paperwork, the dossier process is so in-depth and intense that the modus operandi seems to be to burn you out so completely, and make you so cynical as to not care whether or not the adoption ever happens, and only then do things start to happen. We've been working on our dossier forever. We had a home study once, eons ago, that seemed to take forever to complete. We've notarized copies, copies of copies, and originals. We've been told that our notarizations were no good, and then re-notarized. In the time it's taken us to complete this paperwork, (insert Pro Athlete Name Here) has probably sired at least six more illegitimate children. Irony.

A couple of months ago, on our way up north for a book signing, we received the call from Jennifer, our Bethany caseworker, that Alla (the little girl Jennifer had called us about) had been adopted by a Ukrainian family. Just like that. We drove on in silence for a few minutes, and I knew immediately what the call was about, as soon as I heard Jennifer's tone of voice.

We knew this was very much a possibility. In international adoption, at least ten things seem to go wrong, before one or two things go right. Alla "going right" would have been almost eerily too easy. As such, we tried not to invest too much, emotionally, in her. I remember trying not to pray for her by name, so as to protect my emotions from this phone call. One of my defense mechanisms is to act like I'm not surprised by stuff like this. "I figured this would happen," I told Kristin, as if the foreknowledge of something makes it easier. People who know they're going to die still don't want to.

That night, as if by God's grace, we had a wonderful evening in the hotel with Tristan after the book signing. We watched movies, drank pop, ate pizza, and laughed a lot. I thanked God for my little family in a way I don't think I had before. It's the kind of thankful that makes you want to call your parents, to thank them. You get weepy watching your son splash around in a hotel pool.

The fallout of Alla's being adopted by a Ukrainian family meant that we would in all likelihood be waiting much longer for a child. That hurts even more. 2008 seems tangible. 2009 seems like forever. An adoption that had felt so real and tangible now, again, feels very abstract. And much scarier this time. When we adopted Tristan we felt like we still had other options (read: fertility). There's an all-or-nothing finality to this one that makes it somehow heavier.

◌ ◌ ◌

TRANSCRIPT OF A PHONE CONVERSATION
WE NEVER THOUGHT WE'D HAVE

We'd been waiting almost a year and a half since the beginning of this adoption to submit our dossier, and knew that as soon as the dossier was submitted we'd be officially "in the queue" and would hopefully be only a few months away from meeting our new child. Except that it's never as easy as, say, mailing a packet of papers somewhere, or dropping a packet of papers off. It is Ukraine, where even simple things often seem grotesquely complicated. To wit:

Judy from Bethany: Hi Kristin, it's Judy. (At this point Kristin can tell just by the "Hi Kristin" that Judy has bad news. But still, at this point in the process it's exciting just to see the number for the adoption agency come up on the caller ID.)

Kristin: Hey Judy, what's up?

Judy: Well...

Kristin: ...

Judy: We have some bad news regarding your dossier. (Anytime anyone actually uses the word "regarding" you know it's bad news.) It seems there was an, uh, *altercation*, at the Ministry of Adoption on the day your dossier was supposed to be submitted.

Kristin: ...

Judy: It seems our representative was, sort of, like *accosted* at the front of the line, dossier in hand. So to speak.

Kristin: Like a words-exchanged sort of altercation? Words were had? Voices were raised, et cetera?

Judy: No, as I understand it, it was like a real fight-type altercation. A thug who was there representing another agency pushed his way to the front and sort of "roughed up" our rep.

Kristin: . . .

Judy: And as a result they've closed the Ministry of Adoption and your dossier wasn't submitted.

Kristin: A thug? Really? Roughed up?

Judy: Really. We don't know how long the ministry will stay closed. It could be a day or it could be six months.

Kristin: This is a blow.

Needless to say, this aroused in us a variety of emotions, ranging from anger to wanting to quit the adoption altogether—the adoption in which we'd already invested upwards of $20,000. Judy was a saint in terms of walking us through our options and ultimately advising us to hang in there and stay the course. And for us it was another lesson in quietly trusting a God who was faithful in our first adoption, with all its attendant ups and downs. Further complicating matters was the fact that I'd cleared my teaching schedule for the spring, so as to accommodate a long trip to Ukraine. I would now scramble to piece together a schedule, and income, for that period of time. I also posed the question to Judy: If thugs were needed to escort our dossier to the front of the line, could I, possibly, be that thug? I even explained to her that I could look awfully thuggish, especially when wearing a backwards ball cap or skullcap.

I imagined myself flying to Ukraine, alone, and then when I got there purchasing the requisite Eastern European tough-guy track suit. I imagined shaving my head. I imagined walking up to the front of the line with the Bethany rep, with our dossier, hoping and praying that I wouldn't have to have a go with a thug from another adoption agency—some gold-toothed giant with a head like a slab of beef and hands like sledgehammers. I thought again how laughable and weird our life had become.

◌ ◌ ◌

In a public sense, adoption is hot right now—a phenomenon I hope to take full advantage of vis-à-vis selling this book. It's hot not only in a Brad-and-Angelina celebrity way, but it's also a "hot" topic in our church, which is still cranking out biological children at a breakneck pace. That said, we were somewhat surprised to find an announcement in the bulletin for a quote, "Adoption Informational Meeting," featuring reps from area domestic and international adoption agencies. Apparently there were people at our church who were interested in "learning more" about adoption.

One of the unfortunate things about infertility is that for a period of time it gives you a bad attitude about almost everyone and everything. And while we were initially excited about a church-wide adoption-awareness-raising event, our enthusiasm was quelled when we saw the attendee list on a clipboard[2] in the narthex. Slated to attend the meeting were the handful of cool, successful, huge families that already had a passel of beautiful biological children—families who, it should be added, were and are among our closest friends. Now, far be it from me to somehow get mad because they either wanted to adopt, or wanted to appear like they wanted to adopt, but either way I should be enthusiastic about their enthusiasm . . . right?

The other unfortunate thing about infertility is that you don't really know when your angst is justified, or when you're just being overly sensitive. Is it just rampant oversensitivity and wound-edness that causes us to overthink our attendance at an adoption meeting that was planned for the encouragement and edification of the body? Again, probably.

We didn't go to the meeting. It would have been too hard to sit in the room, which at that point was so full of new babies as to resemble a church nursery. Apparently, there was only one genuinely potential adoptive family in the room—this, of course, according to that one genuinely adoptive family. The rest of the attendees were a smattering of big families and, oddly, a random group of college guys who seemingly attend absolutely every church-sanctioned event regardless of content.

And it's not so much angst over the fact that they want to adopt, or want to want to adopt; rather it's the fact that they have something we want and can't have—biological children—and now they're going to have our thing too.

NOTES

1. I didn't really know what this was before starting the process, and honestly, still don't. I just know that it involves going to "The Office of the Great Seal" and being sassed by bored, unhelpful government-employee types. Which begs the question: Do sassy cranks gravitate toward government work, or does government work make you a sassy crank?

2. This is something church people like: sign-up sheets for everything, on clipboards in the church lobby.

For you did not receive the spirit of slavery to fall back into fear, but you have received the Spirit of adoption as sons, by whom we cry, "Abba! Father!"
—Romans 8:15 (ESV)

I suggest that we cross the line between self-examination and introspection when, in a sense, we do nothing but examine ourselves, and when such self-examination becomes the main and chief end of our life.
—D. Martyn Lloyd-Jones, *Spiritual Depression*

CHAPTER 3:
IS THERE LIFE ON MARS? (TRAVELING, AGAIN)

March 2009

I'm ensconced in a butter-colored leather sofa on the fifth floor of a beautiful little apartment building in a beautiful little section of Kiev. The building and I are about half-a-block's walk from McDonald's, where I had my first meal in Ukraine (chicken nuggets and a Coke). This morning, I asked God if it was wrong to pray that our new child be located in Kiev, simply so that we could continue staying in this apartment, which has a huge, flat-screen television, an American-style whirlpool tub, and a DVD player that plays our DVDs. Also a heated floor in the kitchen. Not that any of that matters, of course. It's about the children.

We're a day or so past a twenty-six-hour travel day that unfolded, thankfully, without adventure. It struck me somewhere over the Atlantic Ocean that we would really be *doing* this trip with Tristan, who is now six years old. He sat next to me on the

Austrian Airlines flight, coloring, or pressing buttons incessantly on the mini-TV in the headrest in front of him. Thankfully (again) he slept for four hours on the flight—his enormous, swelteringly hot head in Kristin's lap, and his big feet alternately kicking me in the head, the ribs, and the crotch. Still, I'm glad he slept.

It occurred to me on the flight that Kid Rock videos appear especially ridiculous when viewed without sound. Because on an international flight you're not only viewing your programming, but the programming of those seated in your immediate vicinity. Seeing Kid Rock in the videos—wiggling his pelvis around, long hair flying, dressed like a cross between Liberace and a gas station attendant—made me feel less than proud to be an American. I also watched a movie called *The Rocker*, which starred Dwight Schrute (Rainn Wilson) from *The Office*, playing, essentially, Dwight Schrute—except this Dwight Schrute used to be a drummer in a rock band and was now dealing with the reality of maturing, as a person, without being a rock and roller. The movie was lame but it made me feel beyond comfortable and sort of *at home*, so I watched it twice.

Tristan was an absolute champ through the transatlantic flight, and a long layover in Vienna, where it appeared that romance was not dead. We spent several hours sitting on stainless steel chairs in a room that seemed to be made entirely out of concrete and glass. It was not unlike a standard basement.

Anyway. A swarthy youngish guy was seated about three stainless steel chair-lengths away from an attractive, young Ukrainian woman in a turtleneck. The guy looked not unlike Shia Labeouf.[1] He looked continually in the girl's direction, while the girl perfected an uncaring pouty-chic look and seemed to be completely enthralled with her cellular device. The guy, who looked a little more, how you say, *hardscrabble*, based on his attire, produced a pen and wrote a note, declaring his love to her on the back of a receipt. And then, when his flight was announced (he's going to Istanbul, she's going to Kiev), he dropped the note in her lap and walked over to get in line. By this time the gate area had begun to fill, she read the note, shaking her head a couple of times, but getting that intrigued/flattered look that girls get when guys are interested in them—even guys to whom they wouldn't normally give the time of day. She glanced in his direction a couple of times, but they happened to be the few times when he wasn't looking at her. He boarded the plane, finally, without ever having caught her eye. They never shared a look. She didn't chase him down the tarmac for a long, passionate kiss. They were never married. We were enthralled by the story, wondering what the note said—a note we even considered stealing at one point, at great risk to ourselves. Instead, common sense won out in both cases—as in typical, no-nonsense Ukrainian fashion, the girl left the note on her seat as she boarded the plane. But, for us, romance was not dead.

◻ ◻ ◻

Getting to this point, to Kiev, had not been without drama. After learning that the Ukrainian adoption program was almost hopelessly stalled, after the altercation at the Ministry of Adoption, we resigned ourselves to more waiting. I booked several speaking engagements, and signed on to teach a semester's worth of college writing courses. It was at this point that things seemed to turn, miraculously, for the better. Figuring I would never finish this book, I emailed Judy, our contact at Bethany Christian Services, asking her what I should tell my editors about the future of the book. Later, that day, she called to tell us that we had an appointment and would be traveling, in four weeks, to Ukraine. "Don't think it's because you emailed today," she said, kindly.

This call came at a great time, partly because we were in the process of making some peace with infertility, and with our church. As could easily be ascertained from earlier in the book, bitterness had become something of an issue and theme for us. We knew it was wrong but at times felt like we couldn't beat it. For a couple of months we even considered leaving our church— hoping to find something a little less, ah, *fertile*. But in spite of the hard feelings we still loved our church and felt conflicted about the decision. So in true American fashion we decided to book a hotel room, call it a "retreat," and go there to pray about our decision and ask God to show us any sin in our hearts. And show us He did. We sat down with a notebook and labeled two columns— one called "Our Sin" and the other called "URC's Problems." Not surprisingly, the Our Sin column was much longer. Once we took the time to sit down, really pray, and unpack all of our thoughts about the issues, the Lord blessed us by showing us a long list of our own shortcomings. We prayed that He would begin to take away these sins, and that He would forgive us. We decided to stay at URC, and do so without the giant chip that had previously been residing on our shoulders. Not that everything immediately became perfect, but we were at least learning to love our church again before leaving for Ukraine.

Learning that we were cleared to travel set off another chain reaction of logistical nightmares, proving that there's never really a good time to leave your life for two months. We had to first arrange financially for the trip—making sure that we had enough money banked to pay our bills stateside, as well as enough credit to finance the overseas stuff. We once again had to pull massive amounts of cash out of the bank, which proved difficult both because of Michigan's death-rattle economy, and the fact that nobody in America uses cash anymore. We ended up having to go to three banks to secure the necessary number of clean $100 bills we needed.

It's during this phase of the process that you realize that preparing to leave is actually worse, and more stressful, than the actual leaving. Holing up in a hovel in Ukraine actually sounds appealing after dealing with the myriad of paperwork, good-byes, expectations, and miscellaneous junk one has to deal with stateside.

We also had to secure another round of papers—most notably a notarized "employment verification letter" that would come from our tax accountant. For the first time in my professional career I've actually hired the services of a tax accountant—in the past these letters have come from an agent, and a friend who sells mortgages but did our taxes on the side. Let me explain how this very important letter works. First, I write the whole thing myself, explaining how I make my money, how much I made last year, and how much I think I'll make the following year. I imagine Ukrainians reading this, and wondering how I make a living writing about boxing, football, pro wrestling, and the church. Sometimes I ask myself the same thing. Next, I email the letter to the accountant, who prints it on his letterhead, signs it, and notarizes it. And then, here's the fun part, he charges me $300 for his trouble. For pressing the "print" button on his PC. Actually, for his secretary pressing her "print" button. He could have at least bought me dinner first.

◻ ◻ ◻

Lesya calls this morning, around 9:30, to tell us to meet her on the street, at the café, in twenty minutes. On the street we all pile into Vadim's Chevrolet and take off for the Ministry of Adoption office. The office is now located in old town, next to a huge, beautiful blue cathedral.

A few things have changed, culturally, since our last visit. For one, the office has upgraded to this building, which is considerably lighter, and more comfortable. And by lighter, I mean it appears that the country has decided to turn their collective lights on, lessening the cave-likeness of the whole place. We settle into a leather sofa, to wait. Once again, Tristan is a champ. We thumb-wrestle, and he plays his Game Boy quietly. "Why are the buildings here so old?" he asks. After a few moments, we're summoned upstairs to meet with the psychologist, who in the duration of a twenty-minute meeting never shakes our hand and hardly looks at us.

We soon learn that a deal has already been made on our behalf, by Lesya, who I'm beginning to admire as a sort of European, female Jerry Maguire character. She's the queen of the meeting room. She makes things happen. Lesya tells us to pretend to look at a pile of files on the coffeetable in front of us. We don't just pretend to look at them, but actually look at them. They all have the familiar, sad-eyed, rough-looking orphanage mug shot on top of files written in Russian. They're all older kids, which makes them tougher to adopt. And they're all, according to Lesya, unhealthy.

She tells us of a young boy, Dmitri, who just turned three. He lives in an orphanage in Kiev, which Lesya tells us is "the best orphanage in Ukraine." Our hearts sink a bit, because we have hoped and prayed for a girl, but we're thrilled that the child is healthy. And then Lesya adds, "And he has a sister." Oh? "She is one year old," she says. "She is not eligible for adoption, but in a year you can come back for her. It is good for you?" I look at Kristin and she looks at me. We decide, without words, that it's good for us.

Lesya explains that they will essentially "hold" Dmitri's sister for us, which means that only her birth mother could potentially come back for her. We'll meet them both, at the orphanage, in forty-eight hours.

After filing out of the office we learn that there is a problem with our paperwork. "This is a very big problem, and you could lose the referral," Lesya says, before scuttling back inside. She's wearing perhaps the most garish white fur coat I've ever seen anyone wearing who's not also in a music video. And like all Ukrainian women she wears long, leather boots with high heels and pointy toes. Still, she glides over the cobblestone sidewalk effortlessly. There is no "casual" in Ukraine, especially for women. If a woman has left her house, it means that she is dressed to the nines in nightclub-ready attire. We look and feel schlumpy by comparison.

Losing the referral means that we could lose Dmitri as quickly as we found him. The problem is with a document that didn't get apostilled, which is another fancy way of saying that you pay a premium to get a stamp[2] on an official document, which makes it "more" official. We stand on a cobblestone street that is thousands of years old, and pray. We know that God is good, and that He's gone before us thus far. We pray that He would go before us in the meetings, and that the powers that be would look kindly on us.

◇ ◇ ◇

We're four days into our trip and already the apartment walls are closing in on us. Simply put, Tristan, the love of our lives, has an innate ability to find our last nerve and then grate on it. He's loud. He's chimpy. He can make a seven hundred-square-foot apartment feel like two hundred square feet. He fills up a room. He's been amazing in public, but in private he's driving us crazy.[3]

"Only fifty-six days left," Kristin says, sarcastically, at breakfast. It's ironic that we've moved heaven and earth to come here to adopt a child, and the one we have and love is driving us crazy.

◇ ◇ ◇

Random observances, from today:

• Beer, it seems, is cheaper than water. A tallboy can of Becks— a German beer that in America is considered a good import—is four grivnas and change, which amounts to about fifty cents. Meanwhile, a two-liter bottle of Evian is twenty-five grivnas.

• I saw a pack of Chesterfield cigarettes for sale today. I thought people stopped smoking that brand after WWII.

• I watched MTV's *Hogan Knows Best*, a reality television program featuring former popular wrestler Hulk Hogan and his dysfunctional family, in Russian. It was lousy in this language too.

• The girl who checks us out at the local market has a certain way of throwing the change and receipt at me that suggests something like: "I hate you and wherever you came from inside the, like, *core*, of my innermost being and I hope I never see you again."

• The bed in our apartment is hideously uncomfortable. It's like sleeping on top of a snare drum. When I flick the top of the "mattress" with my finger it makes a *ping, ping* sound, and most nights I end up on the butter-colored leather sofa. Yes, I'm a wimpy, pampered American. I know this. And realizing that Shane Claiborne[4] slept on a cardboard box under a bridge for a year just, sort of, *because*, makes me feel even more wimpy, pampered, and suburban.

• Re: The bed—it's also really, like, *gritty*, everywhere here. And by gritty I mean that in the streets and on the sidewalks there's a sort of muddy, sandy mixture everywhere that comes into the apartment on one's shoes, and then gets transferred to one's bare feet, and then eventually ends up in the bed where it begins, slowly, to drive me insane when despite all of my best efforts to brush or wipe it away it never really goes away.

• I'm getting used to peeling off large amounts of cash, in the backseats of cars. I paid Irina $6,000 today, in a Volkswagen, outside the Ministry of Adoption. A Ministry of Adoption where, oddly, there seemed to be a parade of American couples signing paperwork. For a country where there are supposedly "no children," there seem to be an awful lot of American families shuffling through here. We ran into a couple from Huntsville, Alabama, tonight, who had that glazed-over "just arrived in Ukraine" look. They're boarding an overnight train for Donetsk, tonight. "We just got settled here," they said, "and now they've got us on the move again." They're in for the ride of their lives. I think this but do not say it. They're an older American couple, who are no doubt used to kind, friendly Southern hospitality, as well as in general being made aware of what is going on. These are two things that just don't happen in Ukraine.

• Regarding a general lack of information: Kristin, my arm-

chair historian wife, hypothesizes that the lousy informa-
tion-sharing that is standard here can be attributed to the old
communist culture, where there really was no sharing of real information. Therefore, Ukrainians have no concept of the idea of
discussing something until all parties feel comfortable. They're
much more comfortable just telling you what to do, and seem to
rather enjoy this.

There's another problem here that seems to have followed us
from the United States—that is, a lack of money. On our previous trip, all travel and lodging-related expenses, like apartments
and drivers' fees, were covered under the flat country fee. This
time, they're out of pocket, and while the accommodations are
much nicer, we do some quick math on day three and realize we'll
run out of money well before we leave if we keep spending at this
rate. Keeping in mind that we're only really spending money on
food, lodging, and being driven to various appointments around
town. The realization of this—the fact that we'll be going broke in
Ukraine—comes as something of a blow at the end of an already
exhausting day.

Our Bethany rep told us time and time again that $18,000
would more than cover all of our expenses while in Ukraine. Now
that we're halfway around the world, this figure is sounding ridiculously low, and I'm pacing a hole in our apartment floor. It's
my first panicky, "I want to get out of here" sort of experience. Up
to this point, the trip had been relatively breezy. We reread the
"travel documents"—which are a cut-and-pasted hodgepodge
mess of random cultural information and travel instructions. But
it says there that $18,000 would be fine, however, their estimates

for drivers' fees ($45 from the airport; we paid $120) and lodging ($45 per night; we're paying $95) have been laughably low. This is a problem. The buttery-leather sofa somehow seems less inviting and comfortable under these circumstances.

Lost in all of this worry is the fact that tomorrow we travel to the orphanage, a thirty-minute drive from Kiev, to meet Dima, our son. At midnight I tell my wife that I can't imagine mustering an emotion other than fear, worry, and rage about the financial situation. We call Lesya to discuss this situation, and she hangs up on us. We wonder if this is cultural—the idea that you're always sort of on a "need to know" basis over here. It's either that, or she hates[5] us.

NOTES

1. This is one thing you'll notice about overseas travel: people look like other people. I saw a guy in the security line in Vienna who looked just like Lou Diamond Phillips, and another guy at a McDonald's who looked just like my buddy JR.

2. This amounts to a dumb, two-dollar State of Michigan sticker.

3. He makes these noises with his stuffed animals, who are either always talking to each other or fighting, and when they're talking to each other they're doing it (talking) in this sort of high-pitched squeal. It's the kind of squeal that makes me want to send him as far away from me as possible.

4. In case you don't know who Claiborne is, he's the evangelical world's current favorite White Guy with Dreads, and wrote a book about how he lived as a homeless person for a year, or something, and now he's a superpopular and in-demand conference speaker, and is sort of a younger, cooler, Jim Wallis/Brian McLaren white-guilt type guy.

5. Lesya is fond of telling us that we're her "favorite couple" to work with, though the more time I spend around her it occurs to me that she must tell this to every couple. Lesya, among other things, is a shrewd saleswoman because this—making someone feel like they're your favorite—is something that all great salespeople have an innate ability to do. And the best ones aren't even, necessarily, lying. The best salespeople, I think, actually believe that everyone is their favorite client, a belief which allows them to constantly be "in the zone," so to speak. There has to be a zen koan in that somewhere.

A bruised reed he will not break, and a smoldering wick he will not snuff out.
—Isaiah 42:3

CHAPTER 4:
PLEASE, GIVE ME A SECOND GRACE: DIMA

One downside to the driver expenses all being out of pocket is that it sucks the joy out of just driving around Kiev, which we do a lot of today. Dima's orphanage is about thirty miles outside the city, which gets much less affluent and glitzy as one works one's way toward the outskirts. The orphanage is in what amounts to a village, but I can tell immediately that it will be scads nicer than the orphanage Tris was from. I make this assessment based on the fact that there are lights on there and someone smiles at us on our way in. Smiling at someone is almost a revolutionary act over here, and it makes a huge difference.

We're led up a narrow staircase and into a playroom, where there are newish-looking tricycles, and a smaller version of a ball pit like you might find in a Chuck E. Cheese in America. And there are lights on. A German couple plays in the room with their adoptive son. They smile, introduce themselves, and shake hands. This lessens the tension considerably.

We're told that Dima will be up in a few minutes, and stake out a spot in a hallway to stand and wait, in front of a fish tank. My parents, in particular, had expressed worry over Tristan's reaction to being in an orphanage setting. They shouldn't have. He has perfected, even at age six, an American nonchalance and stands there chewing gum and making faces at the fish. If this is difficult for him emotionally, he's not showing it.

"Here he is," says Slava, our new guide, with a smile. Slava will handle the orphanage portion of the adoption, and she seems considerably less brusque and cranky than her counterparts. This is a welcome change.

Dima turned three at the end of January, and rounds the corner wearing a pair of what I would later discover are girls' jeans, and a blue sweater with a picture of a monkey on the front. He has a head full of tousled blond hair, and lively eyes. I can tell, immediately, that he'll be a live wire. He looks us over and then heads immediately for the doorknob to a sub-playroom—a big, clean space that Slava tells us is "the music room."

Dima (pronounced Dee-mah) takes about thirty seconds to be shy and then begins flashing a million-dollar smile around the room. A kind, smiling doctor soon enters and leads us through the most comprehensive, sensible conversation we've ever had about adoption in Ukraine. She tells us, basically, everything that has happened to Dima since his birth. She tells us that he was abandoned at a hospital, and had to stay there for the first three months of his life, as is standard here. He's already had the measles and chicken pox. I find myself getting misty-eyed, hearing this information, but feeling incredibly thankful for the good care he's received here.

After the meeting Dima runs to me and throws his arms around my neck. We hug for a while and I tear up, for real, for the first time.

○ ○ ○

There are times in this culture, like this morning when we stepped inside Saint Vladimir's cathedral which is a half a block from our apartment, during which we feel like we could stay here forever. To say that the cathedral was massive, beautiful, and ornate would be a gross understatement. The space was gilded and covered, floor to ceiling, in iconography and candles. It was like something one sees in a movie. There were tourist types, like us, gazing slack-jawed at all of the crosses, mosaics, and paintings, and then there were others there managing to have real religious experiences. I saw a young man standing in front of an altar and breathing deeply. It was clear that he was contemplating something very weighty. There were old women lighting candles in grottos that lined the side walls. I wasn't sure if I was in the presence of God, but I was sure that I was surrounded by a great deal of beauty.

Then there are times when I don't feel like I can stand to be here another day. I remember this feeling well from the first trip, and even from our year living in Lithuania. It's being sick of being stared at. Being sick of the fact that even walking to the kiosk on the corner for a bottle of water turns into a huge adventure. We've been told by Lesya that we will be moving soon, into a cheaper apartment, and have sort of been waiting on pins and needles for Lesya to call and tell us that she's waiting downstairs in a car and that we have five minutes to clean up and pack the apartment.

That's how things work here. There's no advance notice. You have to be ready to move in a heartbeat.

This morning I run the stairsteps in my apartment building, trying to have some semblance of a workout, and trying to do something besides sitting on the butter-colored sofa, thinking ragingly introspective, unproductive thoughts. Later, I read the heights and weights of several NFL linebacking prospects, trying to rescue my brain from self-pitying-type feelings. Brian Cushing, 6'2", 242. USC. Aaron Maybin, 6'3", 245, Penn State. It doesn't work. I read on NFL.com that (then) Broncos quarterback Jay Cutler, in a tiff with management, has put his 5,800-square-foot Denver mansion up for sale, as well as a smaller home in Denver he'd purchased for his parents, though he is keeping his downtown penthouse apartment. I begin to hate Jay Cutler, though we've never met personally . . . but then I realize that reading about Jay Cutler is my entertainment, and in a strange way I'm thankful for him.

The best part of our day happens in the afternoon, when we drive through a sleet storm to see Dima in the orphanage. We're given a private room, with some sofas and toys, to hang out in, and he's soon tearing around the room and jumping off sofas like he has no fear. Dima bonds with Kristin today, which is a relief. Last time he was so enamored with Tristan and me that she was somewhat forgotten, but today he jumps off the sofa and bumps his head, and immediately crawls into her arms for comfort.

The fact that we haven't met Dima's sister is starting to become disconcerting.

◌ ◌ ◌

Wes Janzen is a world-renowned orchestra conductor from Vancouver. He would never describe himself as world-renowned; rather, he explains what he does as "waving my finger around." However, he was the first conductor to stage a performance of Handel's *Messiah* in Germany after the Berlin Wall came down, and has performed in Carnegie Hall and other venues around the world. He also happens to be our neighbor in Kiev, and a vital part of Music Mission Kiev,[1] which is, on paper, an outreach ministry to local musicians but as we find out today, is really much more.

Wes meets me on the street in front of my building, where I tell him, "I'll be there looking hopelessly American." I have no idea, when I meet Wes on the street, that he:

• Lives downstairs from Vladimir and Vitali Klitschko, professional heavyweight boxers who are Ukraine's most famous and successful professional athletes. Wes helped them set up their Christmas tree this year.

• Is a part of a ministry that has led thousands of widows in Kiev to Christ. These are women who lost their husbands to World War II, or Stalin's Gulags. They're women who know the real meaning of hunger, poverty, and hopelessness.

• Would, later that afternoon, introduce us to those women.

• Would take us to church on Sunday, where we would hear a magnificent string orchestra, and a hundred-person Ukrainian choir, praising God.

After a cup of coffee and perhaps the most delicious chocolate croissant I've ever had, at a *patisserie* in our neighborhood, Wes leads us along Shevchenka Street, to a public building that houses the bulk of their ministry. Inside we see a lobby full of old widows lined up to receive a bag of food that includes a package of pasta, some produce, and half a chicken. Many of these women will live off this ration for an entire week and some, Wes tells us, ride public transportation for two hours to get here. The unique thing about these women is that they smile, and there's a joy radiating from their faces that is largely absent in this culture. This is noteworthy in no small part because these women—as old pensioners with no money and no family—are supposed to be the most joyless of Ukrainians. Yet, when they gather to worship and read Scripture there's joy and peace written all over their faces. This is, as you can imagine, both moving and extremely challenging to see in person. Abiding in Christ is more than a mantra for these women. Christ is truly their only hope.

The food operation is a well-oiled machine. Wes's teenage kids, Johnny, Kristina, and CJ, sit behind a counter and hand out bags of food to the women, who are archived and noted on a list. Some of them take multiple bags, which they'll deliver to shut-ins around the city. Many of these women were once leaders in their fields—Wes tells me that one of the pensioners was once Ukraine's top engineer, jailed by Stalin for "something stupid," according to Wes. During her confinement she lost her family and now she is one of Kiev's poorest citizens.

"Our ministry is hurting because of the economy in America," Wes explains, going on to acknowledge that behind every great missionary is, usually, a passel of "rich, entrepreneurial types who believe in the best of capitalism."[2] Though, he says, they're getting the worst of it now, and it's impacting his ministry.

By way of aside, it occurs to me that a sort of bunker mentality happens in a place like this. You become friends with someone simply because you share the same language. For example, we met the Janzens yesterday. Today, we're in their apartment for dinner, and will end up hanging out for several hours. It's refreshing for all of us just to be able to speak English to one another, and trade information on where to buy meat that isn't rancid. We talk about where we've walked in the city. However, the one intangible is the bond that comes with other believers, and the fact that the Janzens do end up being exceedingly cool, funny, interesting people with exceptionally nice kids is a great bonus. We leave their flat feeling beyond blessed to have met them.

NOTES

1. www.musicmissionkiev.org

2. Wes continues by giving a brief thumbnail sketch of the economic history of Ukraine, post-communism. This doesn't pertain to the adoption narrative, per se, but it is nonetheless very interesting. In a nutshell, Ukraine did a complete 180 when communism fell, and there was a very tiny percentage of the population ready to make a massive cash-grab, while the rest of Ukraine stayed very poor. And there's also no concept of personal philanthropy here which, Wes explains, will make the management of Music Mission Kiev by nationals almost impossible. Also, the value of the dollar is plummeting here, so all of the developers and individual borrowers who went crazy when the dollar was strong are taking a beating now.

It ain't much, but it's home.

—Elwood Blues, *The Blues Brothers*

Next time we come here I'm going to ask for a different room.

—Dusty Bottoms, *The Three Amigos*

CHAPTER 5:
MY OWN PERSONAL EL GUAPO: ON COMPLAINING AND NUMBERS 11

It's 11:30 p.m. and I'm staring at a hideously tacky re-creation of Pink Floyd's *Dark Side of the Moon* album cover which hangs in my new living room, as art. Oil on canvas. This is bad enough in and of itself, but it's made worse by the fact that I hate Pink Floyd. If it was a cover of Van Halen's *1984* I would be much more excited. It's illuminated by a curved array of lights that are all the rage here. Curved arrays of lights. Everybody who's anybody has these in their apartments, and they amount to these textured plaster ceiling cut-outs that are affixed to the existing ceiling and are supposed to provide ambience, or whatever. They're all affixed by drilling, too. I'm convinced that there is one power tool produced and used in all of Ukraine, and it's the drill. Somebody, somewhere in our building is always drilling something. I've grown to hate the drill.

I do push-ups in here, on the floor, like a convict doing hard time. I feel like the Robert De Niro character in *Cape Fear*.

Our new apartment (we moved to save some serious cash on rent) is four hundred square feet, tops, and its features include a pitted hardwood floor in which the hardwood is actually popping up in some spots, making it impossible not to trip over or to snag socks on. There's a tiny entryway, then the living room which has one Sovietly-uncomfortable sofa, a tiny kitchen with a dirty stove and a fridge (also dirty), and a television-with-satellite that gets 556 channels (no exaggeration) and they're all bad. I can get the news in Yemen, watch a ton of soccer (which I find boring in every language), and actually watch Al Jazeera,[1] but I can't get an NBA or NHL highlight to save my life. There's a dirty coffeepot and we can find, total, three spoons in the apartment. There's a planter outside of a window filled with around ninety cigarette butts. And as of right now there's no Internet. Excuse me while I go off to rock in the corner, in the fetal position.

Kristin and I cried for the first time on this trip, a little bit, when we saw the new place. It's in a really nice block, next to a tall, glass-and-steel, European bank building with an overpriced[2] American-style steakhouse. But our building is the worst on the block—another cinderblock Soviet-style dwelling. "It's okay for you?" said Irina, our guide, as she dropped us at the apartment, barely staying long enough to open the car door before throwing us out. When a Ukrainian asks "It's okay for you?" what they really mean is "This is where you're going to live for the foreseeable future, and I'm going to leave before you start crying."

◇ ◇ ◇

We're in the village about thirty kilometers outside Kiev, waiting for our driver, Vadim, who has gone inside to do some banking. Except that Vadim, instead of parking, say, in a parking spot along the sidewalk, has pulled his blue Chevrolet sedan up onto the sidewalk in front of the bank. Right in the middle. "You wait here," he says. Okay. We'll wait here. Right in the middle of the sidewalk. The village is rough. There's mud everywhere and aside from rundown, dilapidated shack-houses, the only dwellings are grim, gray Soviet high-rises. The people look sad . . . and the people who don't look sad look angry. I don't blame them.

This is a great time to explain that Vadim[3] is a really nice guy. He speaks broken English but I've learned that he has a fifteen-year-old son, and that his (Vadim's) musical tastes tend toward old eighties hair metal—Guns N' Roses, Metallica, Motley Crüe, Quiet Riot—just like mine, and that after their seminal album *Appetite for Destruction*, Vadim thinks all of GN'R's subsequent work has been disappointing. He likes Eminem but strongly dislikes the rest of rap music. He also, like me, prefers the Rolling Stones to the Beatles. He's a big guy, and he smokes like a chimney—so much so that the constant lugging of baggage that is a part of his job becomes something of a struggle for him.

I'm thinking about all this as the black Lada with the green racing stripe and tinted windows[4] screeches to a halt behind us, and the driver of said Lada begins laying on his horn. All of the random, smoking sidewalk dwellers begin to look in the direction of our car—the keys to which are inside with Vadim. I had a feeling the middle-of-the-sidewalk parking space was a bad idea and that something like this would likely happen. I had just hoped it would happen when Vadim (pronounced Vah-deem) was with us.

A big, older Ukrainian thug extricates himself from the Lada and begins walking around our car, gesturing and yelling, and in one final flourish of anger, he kicks the front left fender. Then he makes for the driver's side door. Oh boy. Here we go. It's on. On the positive side, he looks to be in his mid-forties. Wild shock of gray hair flapping in the breeze. Leather jacket. Probably a smoker. Probably inebriated, which could be a bad thing but will most likely work in my favor. But on the negative side he's probably tough as nails and has friends here who will have his back. Tristan is in the backseat understandably freaking out. Kristin, I know, is praying. If I could apologize to this guy for Vadim parking his car moronically in the middle of the sidewalk, I would, but instead I look around quickly for a tire iron or something else I can use to put a dent in this guy's thick skull. I wonder what it will be like to spend a night or two in a Ukrainian jail. I decide that in lieu of a tire iron I'll just try to tackle him over a knee-high fence and then see what happens. The guy rips the driver's side door open, at which point I yell: "It's not my car! The driver is inside!" No doubt hearing the struggle, Vadim ambles out and the two of them exchange words, heatedly.

Note: there's a cop standing on the front steps of the bank watching this whole thing and doing absolutely nothing.

Vadim slides into the driver's seat and turns on the ignition. Thank You, Lord, for getting us out of here in one piece! And then Vadim simply moves the car off the sidewalk and into a parking space. You've got to be kidding me. We're staying?! I resume my search for a wrench, or some other such blunt, heavy object. "You wait here," he says, and ambles back inside the bank. In my rearview I see the black Lada pull out of its spot and drive directly into the space in the middle of the sidewalk that was vacated by Vadim. All of that because he wanted to park as illegally, and moronically, as we were. Sometimes I think I'll never understand this place.

◇ ◇ ◇

An email, from our reps at Bethany Christian Services, has sent us into a small, midafternoon tailspin. They mentioned that in one of the photographs of Dima posted on our blog, they may have detected one or two of the attributes of Fetal Alcohol Syndrome—a condition that is prevalent in the orphanages over here. We're familiar with FAS inasmuch as we've heard the term and done some preliminary poking around online. And Dima appears, thus far, to be the picture of health—running, jumping, playing, and even doing cognitive/fine motor stuff like puzzles. Not to mention the fact that we're all hopelessly in love with the little guy. We love his smile. We love his laugh. We love his little voice, his nose, his hair, and his wiry little body.

The email, to say the least, is deflating. We're committed—both emotionally and on paper—to Dima now, and there's no turning back, but the email, in conjunction with the apartment, has us feeling a little beat up. We bundle up and pile into our apartment building's elevator, which today smells like urine, but has at other times smelled like a cat's litter box and an armpit. But we're saving thirty bucks a night by staying here.

Our walk through the city presents its own problems. Tristan, our six-year-old, is determined to do his own thing. He thinks it's fun to pinball between Kristin and me on a crowded city street, and alternates between running into total strangers and falling down. He thinks this is all very hilarious. He's wrong. Our blood pressure is soaring. Kristin and I are both glad he's here, and would have missed him terribly if he'd been left at home, but we both feel, now, that he's ruining what would almost be a pleasant trip for us. The work of keeping him alive—that is, making sure he doesn't get hit by a car, either on the street or the sidewalk—is exhausting, especially when he seems so unappreciative of our concern. At our favorite café, named Double Coffee (which we call Coffee Coffee), we order him a cheeseburger, which is actually a giant block of fried cheese, with no meat. He complains through the entire meal and picks at his food.

I should add that we've had some of our best times with Tristan here too. Almost every evening we wedge ourselves, the three of us, onto our hideous leopard-print sofa to watch a movie together[5] on my laptop. These are great times, as are the times we spend exercising together on the floor of the apartment, and playing Uno. He's a sweet kid.

Slava and Bogdan, another driver, meet us down on the street. Bogdan is a friendly young guy and he has a nice car—a little Hyundai SUV of some sort. He also speaks serviceable English. The knock on Bogdan is that he drives like an absolute maniac. Fast and furious. We call his car The Vomit Comet because riding in the backseat always makes me feel like I'm going to throw up. After a few minutes in silence, I ask Slava about FAS, and Dima.

"Oh no, he is healthy," she says. Slava is not a salesperson; rather, she's a social worker in the true sense of the word. So I trust what she's telling me. She continues: "I see this in many children, and your child is healthy. This is a diagnosis and it would be in the medical file." She then calls Tatiana, a doctor from the orphanage, just to double-check and confirm, and directs me toward a few websites where I can view pictures of children with

FAS. Needless to say, her kindness and professionalism are an answer to prayer. We prayed that God would show us mercy and allow us to get good information, and He has done so.

The burden lifted, we'll enjoy a great night with Dima—playing with him for a couple of hours. He'll bond with Tristan tonight, which is something both of us had prayed for earlier in the day, and we'll grow to love him even more.

◻ ◻ ◻

Kristin and I (mostly I) have been feeling convicted about something, of late, and that is our propensity toward complaining. I complain a lot here. A lot of that complaining finds its way onto the page and results in good writing, of the laugh-getting variety. But that doesn't make it right.

I've felt increasingly convicted that complaining is essentially a rejection of God, who is sovereign and sends every circumstance into our lives and intends it for our good (Romans 8:28). I've always said that one of the drawbacks of Reformed theology (which I love) is that it doesn't leave you anyone to be mad at. So when I pace the apartment and rant, I'm pacing the apartment and ranting at God, and suggesting that what He's given us is somehow insufficient.

At the beginning of Numbers 11, we learn that "the people complained about their hardships in the hearing of the Lord" and that later, in verse 4, "the rabble with them began to crave other food, and again the Israelites started wailing and said, "'If only we had meat to eat!'" Later in the chapter, Moses wonders, aloud, what he has done to deserve all of it, that is, to be put in charge of such whiny people.

God had provided food for the Israelites, and He has provided good food for us. We're in a safe apartment with a roof over our heads. Tristan handled the travel like a champ, and we're all completely healthy. When I rant about the dirty sidewalks, or complain that I'm not at home in my comfortable house, I'm doubting God's provision. I'm disappointed in myself that this contentment lesson has been so hard to learn, but I'm thankful that He sent me Numbers 11 today, and pray that He will forgive me for this besetting sin.

◌ ◌ ◌

So is it complaining, then, if/when I am tempted to characterize much of the city of Kiev as filthy and disgusting? I say that not because it doesn't have beauty—on the contrary it is full of beauty, both geographical and architectural. The filthy and disgusting part is more of a like, *feeling*, of being somehow trapped inside a giant ashtray. Imagine yourself inside a giant ashtray. Can you do this? I can. Both sets of grandparents were smokers. Nearly every square inch of street and sidewalk in Kiev is covered with years' worth of discarded cigarette butts. And those inches that aren't covered with cigarette butts are covered with mud—because every square inch of nonbuilding-ed real estate in Kiev becomes something of a de facto parking space. People park everywhere, making grass an afterthought. There are no, sort of, *expanses*, of green grass. It's expanseless.

I'm seeing all of this from the passenger's seat of Bogdan's Hyundai crossover, where I'm convinced I'm going to die. Bogdan drives like a maniac. He drives as though the laws of traffic and physics don't apply to him and does it with a demented half-grin on his face. I both love him and hate him for this.

After riding in the car with Bogdan, it's common to spend the rest of the evening feeling sick. "I wish I could just telepathically make a handful of Tums appear in my hand, and then in my stomach," I tell Kristin.

"There are some in your bag," she replies. I cock an eyebrow, which indicates that I would be forever indebted to her if she would make the Tums appear in my hand.

"I'll get them for you," she says.

"You're a doll."

She is a doll. Much like Dima's sister is a doll. We met her today at the orphanage, where she was brought into a room, bleary-eyed and crying, after being woken up from a nap. She had a headful of blonde hair in pigtails, which made her look not unlike Cindy Lou Who from the Dr. Seuss book *How the Grinch Stole Christmas.* She was adorable.

However, part of my stomach problem lies in the fact that I have absolutely no idea how I'm going to pay for her adoption, because, honestly, I really sort of have no idea how I'll pay for Dima's. There's a fine line between faith and stupidity, fiscally speaking, and sometimes I fear that I have crossed or am crossing that fine line.

◻ ◻ ◻

It's alternately raining/sleeting/snowing today, which in America we would call a "wintry mix." This particular wintry mix started sometime in the middle of the night and has persisted through the late afternoon. I checked the ten-day forecast online and it's going to be this way for the next eight days. No sun. I almost wept. Needless to say, the walls of the apartment are beginning to do a little bit of closing in. We need to get Tristan out for a walk, in spite of the weather, or we run the risk of all going insane by late evening.

On the walk—a walk that, by the way, is extremely wet and cold, a kind of seepy, pervasive wet/cold—I am occupying the spot on the sidewalk closest to the road when a car comes racing by, sending a stream of filthy, freezing cold puddle water flying up into my face and all over my right side.

"I hate this country!" I shout, to no one in particular. Fortunately there's no one around (see: horrible weather). We walk on.

"I know this is hard for you to believe," Kristin says, "and it's hard for me to even articulate why . . . but I really kind of like it here."

" . . ."

She slips into a kiosk for a minute to buy some Coke Light (Diet Coke) and grape juice. The fact is that I both enjoy and appreciate Kristin more here, in Ukraine, which presents something of a silver lining in this whole frustrating process. The fact is that I need her to keep me afloat emotionally and that the presence of her is, I understand more acutely here, something of a gift from God.

I spend more time just looking at her here. I spend more time holding her. Sometimes, in the evenings we'll just sit on the couch in each other's arms, and I'll forget how much I hate the couch and how much I want to go home. I'll even, sometimes, wish we could hold each other, in this suspended state of reality, forever. She's beautiful. I like her smile and her sense of adventure. I like that we can spend literally every waking moment together and not get tired of each other. We've been married twelve years and have been, to some degree, to hell and back with the infertility. We have twelve years' worth of inside jokes. I tell her at least three times a day here that I couldn't do this without her. I thank God for her.

"Please do."

"Please do what?" she asks.

"Articulate why you like it here."

◻ ◻ ◻

Money, and the process of adopting Dima's sister remains an issue here. We've only told our families of the presence of Olga, but they have fixated on it, and on the possibility of bringing her home on this trip. We've been trying to prepare them for the fact that such a possibility simply doesn't exist for the following reason: the lengthiness of this adoption program has everything to do with the fact that the Ukraine wants us here for two months so that it can pump us out of more American dollars. That's it. We have friends adopting from China (ten days) and even Ethiopia (two weeks). There's no reason we need to be here for two months, besides the fact that we'll be opening our wallets early and often. Even in the face of the miracle that is Dima—a healthy, younger boy than we could have imagined—it's still hard for resentment not to set in.

And we're worried that if we don't come home with Olga this time (we won't), that our families will be let down or disappointed. We don't want them to see Dima as a means to Olga, and want them to recognize Dima for the miracle that he is, in and of himself. We thank God for Dima, and we thank God for the relative ease of this process so far, and for the fact that I hate it here considerably less than I did last time, and even considerably less than I did a couple of weeks ago when we arrived.

Part of our perspective on money and our relative comfort has come from the Janzens and their ministry. They have become good friends, and our times with them have become—in addition to the visits with Dima—the highlights of our weeks. Today, as we walked to the Dnipro River, which cuts through the center of Kiev and provides some truly breathtaking views, Kim told us the stories of three Ukrainian children in their church. One, Viktor, was raised until age eight by an alcoholic mother who would beat him if he didn't come home with money. One day she burned their home down and little Viktor escaped to the Kiev train station, where he lived until he was taken into foster care. Another, Nastya, lost her eighteen-year-old brother after he became intoxicated and froze to death on the family's front porch. Yet another child—a sweet, six-year-old girl suffering from general parental neglect—fell six stories out her flat window and survived with minimal injuries and no brain damage. Stories like this, sadly, are a dime a dozen in Ukraine and help us as we put our own struggles in perspective.

At the same time, we're all three dealing with our relative spoiledness. I wake up from a nap this afternoon to find Tristan sucking on a microphone that we use to Skype our family, when he was supposed to be watching *Spongebob Squarepants*—which, incidentally, I think is the most worthless piece of junk on kids' television. I think the creator of Spongebob should be forced to live in a four hundred-square-foot flat with a six-year-old "fan" and then see how he likes it.

The trip is wearing on all of us. There has been cloud cover, gloom, and rain for the last eight days, making outside play diffi-cult. This makes just living, for me, difficult. Kiev makes me want to stay in bed all day. I'm reminded of C. S. Lewis's description of hell in *The Great Divorce*—a place where it never stops raining and everyone is miserable. Sounds a lot like here.

NOTES

1. Which I had been led to believe was all hostage-situation videos and terrorist mes-sages.

2. "Big Meat business lunch—ninety grivna."

3. Another random fact about Vadim: every time he stops the car for any reason—like a stoplight—he applies the parking brake. So he's constantly cranking on that big handle between the two front bucket seats. I don't know anything about cars, but that can't be good for it.

4. The American equivalent to this kind of tricking-out of a car would be a souped-up Chevette, or maybe a Ford Pinto. Ladas are Soviet-era junk.

5. Other things we watch together, and get a kick out of, together: YouTube clips of Will Ferrell as legendary USC strength coach Chuck Barry; clips of Chris Farley as Matt Foley, motivational speaker; and my personal favorite—clips of Ferrell doing his Harry Caray impersonation.

I see a red door and I want it painted black.
—The Rolling Stones

How long, O Lord? Will you forget me forever? How long will you hide your face from me?
—Psalm 13:1

The Christian is never meant to be carried away by his feelings, whatever they are. Never.
—D. Martyn Lloyd-Jones, *Spiritual Depression*

CHAPTER 6:
EXILE ON ZHILIAN'SKA STREET

Apparently Ukrainians never eat, drink, or have to use the bathroom. That's just one thing I learned today—a day that I spent wedged into the back of Vadim's Chevrolet with Kristin and Tristan.

The day began with a cellphone call from Slava, letting us know that she would be picking us up in three minutes. Three minutes! Thanks for all the notice. This trip, ostensibly, was to go to Dmitri's birthplace to sign a document. However, after driving an hour through congested Kiev, and then out through a bunch of little villages, we arrived at the building and were told we weren't needed. We turned the car around and then drove an hour back the other way, then back through Kiev to the Pepto-colored building in an alley, next to a hubcap place, that houses the judge who will try our case. We waited there for another half hour, only to find that we could go back to the apartment. We weren't needed at all. I wanted to put my fist through something. Kristin missed her expat women's Bible study and the widows' knitting group, just so that we could sit in the back of Vadim's Chevy all afternoon. Finally, after several hours, we asked to go to the bathroom. They rolled their eyes and immediately started arguing with each other in Ukrainian, as though the idea of pampered Americans who eat and drink, and therefore have to use bathrooms, is the most ridiculous, inconvenient thing they'd ever encountered.

This was after a sleepless night in which I stayed up until 3 a.m. literally hating my own life. I mistakenly checked the ten-day forecast on Weather.com and found . . . ten more days of gloom and rain. I gave in to the urge to just sit around the apartment and feel sorry for myself, which I did, all night. I Skyped both parents and complained. I woke Kristin up and complained. I explained that I didn't know how I was going to survive one more day here, much less twenty. I raged at Ukraine, bureaucrats, the weather, and God. I raged at infertility, which had technically gotten us into this mess for a second time. I resented the cup God had given us.

My mom told me that I needed to give it over to the Lord and tell Him how I was feeling. "I'm telling you," I replied. "What's the difference? He knows." He does know, technically, but I had stopped praying. Or I at least stopped believing it even though there were little piles of "stones," indicating God's faithfulness, all over this trip, including the smooth travel in, and the relatively efficient path to court. Circumstances weren't the problem. The problem, unfortunately, was getting out of bed in the morning.

I told her that my life—even before the trip—had become

somewhat joyless. I felt constantly burdened by my responsibility to earn and provide; always feeling like whatever I did wasn't enough. This feeling has been underscored by this trip—in Ukraine it's starkly apparent that money makes things happen. It's this way everywhere, but it's especially true here.

"I don't look forward to anything anymore," I told her, thinking specifically of how the thrill of the chase, writing-wise, always used to keep my fire stoked. I was always hungry for the next idea—the next book, the next screenplay, and the next deal. But there were no ideas on the horizon that excited me enough to cover the dread of the editing process—a process that always manages to suck most of the joy out of the writing experience.

She read me psalms and for the first time in my life I wasn't moved.

○ ○ ○

"I love you, O Lord, my strength. The Lord is my rock and my fortress and my deliverer, my God, my rock, in whom I take refuge, my shield, and the horn of my salvation, my stronghold. I call upon the Lord, who is worthy to be praised, and I am saved from my enemies" (Psalm 18: 1–3 ESV).

"Court is an informality," Slava explains. "It will take five minutes." She meant to say "a formality," but I get her drift. We pull up in front of the Pepto building, where it looks like the whole world has converged on a Friday morning. We've sat, and waited, in front of this building many times, but this morning we'll actually go in to testify before a judge for the right to adopt Dima.

We're led into a dim entryway, through a metal detector, and then up a dim staircase, to a larger, even dimmer waiting room with doorways to the respective judges' chambers. In Simferopol, for Tristan's adoption, we were led into an actual courtroom and made to sit next to the rebar cages that held prisoners. Here, apparently, we'll "go to court" in an office. Of eleven potential overhead lights in the large room, only four are working. The room is packed with people, some of whom are sitting around big tables, but most of whom, like us, are standing and waiting. Slava is efficient and courteous, but I'd never call her chatty. In America, small talk would be made to fill these silences, but in Ukraine, we just wait. Tristan, to his credit, is a champ.

Funny, randomly Ukrainian aside: as we're standing and waiting, not making small talk, Slava is sifting through some documents. "Oh," she says, "Dima's sister is not named Olga." Kristin and I both raise our eyebrows and remember the fact that none of the orphanage workers called her Olga, which we both thought odd. "Her name is Anastasia." We smile at each other, knowing that this little gaffe is quintessentially "Ukrainian adoption" and proof of how little we know here. We don't even know the names of our potential children. We also smile because Anastasia is considerably less hideous, name-wise, than Olga.

Finally, we're waved into the office, where a female judge, built like an offensive guard, is perched behind a desk. She wears the traditional judge's robe, along with what looks like an Olympic gold medal around her neck (it isn't). I stand and recite my name, birth date, and address, and Kristin does the same. She asks us a few questions, and then motions for Tristan to come over. We both swallow hard. But she smiles and tousles his hair as he leads her through a photo book of our house, family, etc. She seems delighted, and her offensive-guard-ish countenance softens considerably. She tells Slava that "now we are officially Dima's parents," and that we will wait ten days for custody. Inside we praise God.

◠ ◠ ◠

We return to the apartment, to a power outage. Kristin accidentally craves a cup of tea, and accidentally turns on the teapot at the same time I'm online checking email. Silly her. The apartment goes black, and soon I'm standing on a chair in a pitch-black hallway[1] fiddling with wires that look like they maybe haven't been fiddled with since Stalin.

I'm on the phone with my interpreter, who basically says, and I quote, "Just start pushing buttons." I start pushing buttons, and nothing works. Finally, I find a crusted-over switch, behind a bunch of wires. Kristin is holding the elevator door open, which provides light while I work. Finally I'm able to budge the crusty switch, and we have light. More importantly, we're able to gather on the sofa to watch episodes of *The Cosby Show*, courtesy of the Janzens.

These wind-down times in the evening have become invaluable, and are a great time to bond as a family. We all crash together on the sofa, snuggled in by one another out of necessity.

◠ ◠ ◠

The three cups in my apartment runneth over, and we're praising God from whom all blessings flow. Today we get to play outside with Dima, for the first time! It's so wonderful to be out of the sauna-like playrooms, and away from the judgmental eye of one of the head nurses, who we nicknamed Negative Nelly.

The orphanage actually has a really nice playground in back, with multiple slides, swings, and gazebo-type things, and soon Dima and Tristan are chasing each other around, climbing up and down the slides, and doing regular big brother/little brother stuff. Tristan spots the wide-open spaces and tears off as fast as his chimpy, little legs will take him. He's like an animal uncaged. It makes my gray, old cynical heart just about burst with joy. When we met up today, Dima immediately ran to his big "*bratik*" (brother) and gave him a hug. He smiled when he saw all of us, and we had a truly epic time playing outside. Kristin and I said "Ya lublu, Dima" in our broken Russian, which means, "I love you, Dima."

○ ○ ○

Our other child, however, is another story. We knew, coming in, that we would deal with his noise and exuberance. These aren't sin issues; rather, they're little-boy issues. What we weren't prepared for though, was the sassy attitude, the argumentativeness, and the overall lack of respect for us. He's made an already challenging situation infinitely more challenging.

It gets so bad today that we consider canceling plans we had made to go to the circus, for him, in Kiev. His attitude was so defiant during the day (example: refusing to hold our hands in a crowded street, where he could get run over) that we dragged him home, crying.

The circus itself is one of the most surreal things I've ever seen. One ring, in the middle of a small arena, with a live orchestra. There were random animal acts of various kinds—for example, a pig chasing a stuffed rabbit being pulled in a wagon, by a dog. Cats jumping through rings of fire, in pursuit of mice.[2] Porcupines doing whatever it is that porcupines do. Lions being whipped, prodded, and fed chunks of raw meat. A tiger eating a piece of raw meat out of the mouth of a beautiful woman. I could go on and on. It goes without saying that none of this would be even remotely allowed in America due to animal-rights legislation. The performers, though, were extremely talented—great tumblers, gymnasts, high-wire acts, and horsemen. The whole thing was ridiculously, profoundly entertaining, probably because we were so starved for entertainment and escape. Most importantly Tristan loved it, and I loved sitting in my seat, watching my son laugh.

□ □ □

The electrical problems in our flat have become hazardous to our health. Tonight, at the end of an especially trying day in which various, say, *marital* pressures have been mounting, we lose power again.[3] It's dark as night outside, and even darker in our flat. I curse the flat, the city, and humanity and then stumble to the kitchen to grab the chair I've been using to manipulate the crusty old switches and wires in the hallway. The same hallway that smells alternately of wet dog and bathroom. It's truly one of the grossest places on earth.

The way this typically works is that Kristin will go into the hallway and open the elevator door which, conveniently, shines light right on the fuse box. I'll then poke around in the fuse box, trying to identify and uncrust the proper switch. Tonight I flip that switch . . . and nothing happens. Check that, the lights flicker. I found before that if I jiggle a certain wire, the power will come back on. I jiggle that wire, and feel a hot, searing pain shoot through my right arm. I let out an audible scream and fall off the chair. This is what it feels like to be mildly electrocuted. Strike that off my list of things to do before I die.

The upshot is that the power came back on, after it first shot through the right side of my body. I literally crawl[4] back into the apartment and begin to regain feeling in my arm, which feels like an arm feels when one has hit one's funnybone—sort of tingly and sensitive for a while. I'm looking for sympathy, like a hug or something, but Kristin immediately picks up the cellphone and dials Lesya, who assures her that "this is perfectly normal in Ukraine," and "even children know how to use the fuse box." This nice, soft touch of customer service doesn't help.

I am sitting on the sofa doing an amazing job of complaining, and feeling sorry for myself, which I've been doing all day. Really all week. It's reached its zenith tonight, with the electrocution. I've run out of cusswords to string in front of the word "Ukraine." My vocab is exhausted. I'm looking for sympathy from my wife who, I can tell, is angry at me.

She begins to tell me, in no uncertain terms, that I've treated her poorly the last few days. I begin to cry because she is absolutely right, and justified, in telling me this. The truth hurts. This rebuke, though painful, is necessary and probably long overdue. The fact of the matter is, I've been a huge jerk here, and it's taken every bit of restraint on Kristin's behalf not to have told me about it before now.

"When you rant about Ukraine I feel like you're ranting at me," she says. "And when you walk ten feet in front of me on the side-walk,[5] I just feel stupid and alone." Wow, I've managed to alienate the one person in Ukraine I love more than any other, and on top of that, the only person here who really cares about me.

I apologize and we cry together. We've needed it (the cry). I'm not really a crier but it feels great to do this together. And for the first time in weeks, we make time to really talk.

"What is it, exactly, about this place that you hate so much?" she asks. I think for a moment before responding.

"There are two components to it," I reply. "One is the pervasive filth. The fact that people don't care enough about—*creation*—to not litter it with cigarette boxes, beer bottles, and trash. There's trash everywhere. The trash gets me down. Included when I say 'pervasive filth' is also the weather—the fact that it's been thirty-eight degrees, gray, and sleety every day since we got here. Because of communism, people feel no ownership of anything, therefore they feel no particular compulsion to keep anything clean or looking nice. They see a plot of grass and think 'I could park my car there' instead of thinking 'That grass looks nice.' I hate this.

"The other part of it, and perhaps the most telling or revealing part," I continue, "is the fact that every time I step out of my apartment I feel a massive weight of financial failure. Every time I step into a dark, urine-smelling hallway, I think to myself 'This isn't what I envisioned for my wife and son. I should have made more money so that I could get us into a better, safer, nicer, more comfortable place.' So basically every time we leave the flat and have to encounter the relentless onslaught of filth, mud, garbage, smell, and rudeness that awaits us in Kiev, I feel as though I've failed as a provider."

She understands, and for the first time in a long while I feel like we're really communicating. And in the process of this I realize that I am the Israelites—as quickly as God blesses me (see also: court, Dima, the circus, friends, a church), I forget about it and commence griping.

And for the first time I understand the massive weight she's been carrying, dealing with the irrationality of a six-year-old, and dealing with the irrational, horrible attitude of her thirty-three-year-old husband.

◇ ◇ ◇

"'I am what I am'—whatever the past may have been. It is what I am that matters. What am I? I am forgiven, I am reconciled to God by the Blood of His Son upon the Cross. I am adopted into God's family, and I am an heir with Christ, a joint-heir with Him. I am going to glory." —D. Martyn Lloyd-Jones

Today I lay on my bed and cried for about an hour. This was after losing power in the apartment, twice, and then losing hot water. We have a load of filthy laundry marinating in the washing machine, and no hot water with which to clean it, and no hot radiators upon which to dry it. I was listening to Mark Mothersbaugh on the iPod and reading *Spiritual Depression* by D. Martyn Lloyd-Jones—a book that previously, honestly, had done nothing for me. Today, though, it was as though God put it in front of me just to pull out my soul and speak to it. I read and cried—convicted of my massive sins against not only Kristin and Tris, but God.

Later that day I Skype-chatted with my pastor-friend Cory:

"I feel broken and contrite. This place is breaking me down and kicking my tail . . . but I feel like God is using it. *Spiritual Depression* is speaking to me . . . I laid on my bed and read it this afternoon and cried . . . and I don't really do that, per se. I feel like the malaise that has been my experience for a long time may be giving way to brokenness . . . a good kind. A kind of powerlessness that says 'I've tried and done everything I can to make this bearable and failed' and 'If I'm to find peace and contentment it will only happen in Christ.'"

"Hmm . . . those are good words," Cory said. "It sounds like God is increasing your faith. When you say 'experience for a long time' do you mean since arriving in the Ukraine or extending back before that?"

"Probably extending back before, now that I think of it—especially in the weeks/months leading up to the adoption, as the pressures mounted. I've basically been morbidly preoccupied with myself for a long time . . . and I just pray that God would redeem the years that the locusts have eaten, so to speak.

"I was telling Kristin last night that every time I step outside my door here—into a foul-smelling dark hallway, and then out into a muddy, dirty street—I feel failure. I feel like a financial failure. I feel, acutely, my failure to impregnate Kristin. I resent. Only God can forgive me of that, and only God can give me contentment in this place."

"I'm getting the sense that God had an appointment with you in this place at this time that you did not (could not) anticipate," Cory said. "That this trip is about His work for and in you in multiple ways: building your family, providing you with literary content, and most importantly taking you to the next level of being the man He wants you to be."

"I hope so, man," I replied. "That would make it feel so much more worthwhile . . . and it's only in that—sanctification—that I find my hope these days. Trying to consider the trials pure joy, as they say in James."

Corey responded, "A Scripture that's been particularly meaningful to me lately is in 2 Corinthians where Jesus says to Paul, 'Power is perfected in weakness.' I've found a lot of hope in that statement."

"Most definitely," I replied. "I've thought about that passage a lot over here . . . sometimes I don't think we understand weakness until we're actually, literally, WEAK. I am weak here. I'm not smart, I'm not funny, and I have no ability to effect change of any kind. But that said, I don't want to 'waste' my exile here, in a sanctification sense. I guess if God has business to do with me here, He'll do it."

"You might be experiencing what has forever kept me from wanting to go to a place where I don't speak the language," Cory said. "I feel like my ability to use language is my greatest tool, asset, weapon, and that without it I'm utterly impotent, defenseless, and at the mercy of anyone who might wish me ill. And I'll look like an idiot. Is that about how it feels being an English-speaker in Ukraine?"

"Yes, exactly," I said. And later, we chatted about the book industry, and Paul's testimony—that is, Christ's power being perfected in Paul's weakness.

"But yes, Paul is my model too. He's my hero, really, for a lot of reasons. A big part of it is that the guy was so clearly outrageously talented but had such massive insecurities (both on display big-time in 2 Corinthians). But his insecurities themselves became assets because they became the window for him to see God's sufficiency and grace, from which he received the boldness to be all that he was supposed to be. He really, truly could and did brag about his weaknesses and brag about the Lord because he had a clearer view both of how pitiful he was in himself and how adequate he was in Christ."

I end the chat, feeling encouraged, but hoping God somehow redeems the wasted days, weeks, months, and years that I've spent in complete self-centeredness, if not outright rebellion. I'm encouraged by Lloyd-Jones, quoting from Joel, and I pray that the Lord would restore the years that "the locust hath eaten."

"He has promised to do it; He can do it. The wasted years, the barren years, the years that the locusts and the canker-worms and the caterpillars and all these things have devoured, until there was nothing apparently left, of them He says: 'I will restore to you the years that the locust hath eaten'" (Lloyd-Jones).

NOTES

1. There are lightbulbs in the hallways, but none of them ever work. Ever. This is massively frustrating to me.

2. This is as fantastic as it sounds. Why is it so funny to see cats doing crazy stuff, like jumping through fire? Animal-rights people, feel free to stop reading now.

3. We lose power every time we try to do laundry.

4. Crawling is unpleasant here—as you can imagine, the floors are less than clean.

5. It should be noted that I didn't exactly do this to be a jerk, rather, I was just trying to get Kristin and the kids through the traffic quickly and safely, because getting hit by a car is always a very real possibility in Ukraine.

A wife of noble character who can find? She is worth far more than rubies. Her husband has full confidence in her and lacks nothing of value. She brings him good, not harm, all the days of her life.

—Proverbs 31:10–12

CHAPTER 7:
I WAS MADE FOR LOVING YOU BABY, YOU WERE MADE FOR LOVING ME

My wife has put up with so much here. For starters, she dealt with two weeks' worth of incessant complaining, from me, at the beginning of the trip. She's dealt with Tristan's wild swings of behavior—one minute he's a kind, compliant, even occasionally thoughtful child, and the next minute he's a pulsing chatterbox full of sass and dumb, six-year-old logic. Though I love him dearly, I've decided that the six-year-old boy is the single most challenging people-group on earth. But she's handled it all with a beauty and grace that has made me love her even more, here, than I thought possible. She is truly a gift from God and I was, as the song goes, made for loving her. And thankful that she still loves me.

For me, this trip has been a struggle to control, for lack of a better term, my feelings. I seem to have been at their mercy for most of the trip. If I happen to wake up in a good mood in the morning (rare, at the beginning), it only takes a few less-than-perfect circumstances to change it. Lloyd-Jones says, wisely, in *Spiritual Depression*, "Do not spend too much time feeling your own pulse, taking your own spiritual temperature, do not spend too much time analysing your feelings. That is the high road to morbidity." It certainly has been, in my case. He says, on happiness, "If you break God's laws and violate His rules you will not be happy. If you think that you can be a Christian and exert your own will and follow your own likes and dislikes, your Christian life is going to be a miserable one."

We're in the midst of strange days here. We've been to court and been granted permission to adopt Dima, but are waiting ten days until he can stay with us. And, to make matters more frustrating, he's sick in the orphanage and we're not allowed to see him. All of this is on my mind as I walk through Kiev to meet Kristin at the Music Mission Kiev widows' knitting group. I can count on one hand the number of times I've seen the sun in Kiev, but today is one of the times, and as I walk through the large central park in the city, I realize there are things about this I'll miss. It sort of feels like the feeling you get as you near the end of summer camp—you wouldn't necessarily want to do it again—the uncomfortable cots, bad food, sleep deprivation, and the like—but there are certain almost indefinable things you'll miss.

One of those things is the widows' ministry. It's tangible, visible proof of Christ's transforming power, as these women literally have nothing material to be happy about. They've all lost their husbands. They've got no money and barely enough food to eat. Yet, unlike the rest of Kiev, there is joy in their countenances and peace in their hearts. I can honestly say that I share in their joy, but I also feel ashamed of many of my thoughts and behaviors in Kiev as they share their testimonies. They weep with joy recounting receiving their first Bibles. They speak of confinement to orphanages as children, and imprisonments as adults. It's all very sobering, but they're also happy in a cheek-pinching, candy-offering, grandmotherly way that also lifts my burden considerably. The existence of them—in this dark, frowning, mostly joyless city—reaffirms my faith in the existence of a loving, powerful God who is "faithful and just to forgive us our sins and to cleanse us from all unrighteousness" (1 John 1:9 ESV).

One of the women approaches me, weeping, after hearing our adoption story. She was once an orphan and was touched by our story. We're visited also by a man with Down syndrome, who is also crying, and gives our family a big hug, communicating all he needs to communicate without words, and despite a huge language barrier. These events move me more than I will ever be able to communicate on the page. They move me in a way that touches my heart, points my attention back toward a loving God, and also challenges the lack of perspective and the tendency to complain that has dogged me here.

◌ ◌ ◌

Speaking of (complaining) we've spent another entire day in the car. This is one of those days, in life, that you look back on and realize that it's just gone. We met Slava and Vadim at 8:30 a.m. at our apartment, and promptly drove to the Pepto building (courthouse) where we sat in the backseat of the car for two hours. "You wait here," Slava said, as she exited the vehicle. Vadim read the owner's manual and smoked Marlboro Reds. We sat in back and tried to ignore the fact that we really, really needed a restroom. He called Slava and barked something into the phone, and then took us, literally, two hundred meters down the street to a beautiful Shell station, with a market and a clean bathroom. We could have walked there a hundred times and back.

From there, we drove on to Boyarka, where Dima lives, to pick up another piece of paper. We waited another hour in the car while it drizzled outside. The highlight of this stop was being able to go into an Apteka (pharmacy) and buy a sippy cup for Dima. It's the little things. Without a word to us, Vadim sashayed over to a kiosk and bought a hot sandwich. It would have been nice, potentially, to have known that leaving the car to buy a sandwich was an option. It occurs to us that we're not paying them to be friendly or helpful. We've gotten a referral for a wonderful child and, in their minds, that's it.

From there it was on to a notary in Kiev, which was barely two blocks from our apartment. "You wait here." More backseat waiting. By this time Tristan was climbing the walls. And, oddly, we discovered that we were waiting in front of the same bar where we waited and were sick to our stomachs for several hours at the end of Tristan's adoption. Ahh, the memories.

The thing is, they don't tell you anything here. They don't say, for example, "This might take an hour so feel free to go into the bar and get a sandwich or a cup of coffee." Instead, we ate Snickers bars and drank pop that came out of our backpacks. The highlight of this wait was the fact that a giant city pigeon landed on Vadim's car and did what pigeons do (see also: it being the little things).

We were doing all of this paperwork, ostensibly, so that we would be ready to pick up Dima tomorrow, but at the notary's office we learned some troubling news. Apparently the computers, not for the office, but for the entire city where Dima was born, are down. The whole city is down. Therefore, no birth certificate, so no picking up Dima. Cue white-hot rage. "This was going too smoothly," I told Kristin. "Something quintessentially Ukrainian—like the president instituting a random holiday, or the computers for the entire city going out—was bound to happen. This is that thing."

When we finally get to Dima's birthplace, we're led into a large public building that provides the centerpiece for the entire town. One of the disadvantages to building all of your buildings out of cement is the fact that all of the shoddy wiring happens on the exteriors of the walls inside the structure. The advantage is that your buildings would survive the hypothetical tornado that happens once a decade here. The downside is that whenever somebody accidentally brushes one of the wires, walking by, the whole town might lose its computers.

"Hard to believe the computers went out here," I say to Kristin, sarcastically, gesturing at a bundle of old, exposed wires sticking out of a wall. We're led up a staircase and through, literally, a door made out of rebar. A prison type of door. We then sit in a hallway on discarded theater seats while the last of the document is typed up. Out of the next door come the sounds of a community choir practice of some type. We can hear the conductor imploring them to "crescendo!" in Ukrainian, and both realize that almost all conductors are unintentionally hilarious.[1]

"The director is very meticulous," says Slava, who has come out into the hallway to check on us. "She wants to get everything right." It's 6:45 p.m., well past quitting time. Finally, we're led into the director's office, where she offers us tea and cake. For the first time, Slava opens up a little bit and we have a great conversation about what it was like for her growing up in Kiev. The director is delightful as well. She thanks us profusely for adopting one of their own, and says, in her broken English, that we're "very courageous" and that "God will bless" us. At the end of a marathon day, her touch of human kindness is exactly what we need.

◠ ◠ ◠

They're not big on ceremony here, in the Boyarka orphanage. We were required to provide a bottle of champagne and a box of chocolates for both the orphanage director and the head nurse, and didn't get to deliver either of those in person. They were delivered by someone else, in plastic bags—the kind that are free in America at the grocery store, but that you have to pay for here. We were also required to provide candy and juice for the other kids for a celebration that none of us would get to see or be a part of. There's a big metaphorical curtain here, that we never get to see behind and, truth be told, we probably don't want to see behind.

"It's like jail for little kids," says a friendly, astute Israeli man who is here with his wife adopting another toddler. "They live their whole lives in three rooms, and they only get to go outside for twenty-five minutes a day, if it's nice." We both shake our heads, an Israeli and a Michigander, in agreement. Who would have thought? We both shake our heads at the extent to which they insist Dima be bundled up before he goes outside, for the last time. It's sixty degrees and sunny outside, yet he's dressed like he's going for a hike at the North Pole.

We sign a book and, just like that, walk to the car with Dima. No pomp, no circumstance. I hope the girls enjoy their champagne.

There's something mind-blowing about seeing someone have their little three-year-old mind blown for the first time. Dima has lived in a world that has literally consisted of three rooms and a small playground. Kiev is a wonderland for his little eyes. He spends the rest of the afternoon with his eyes glued to the car window, pointing out "machinas" (cars) and "autobuses" all afternoon.

Regarding the rest of the afternoon, it's a funny look at the Ukrainian paperwork process. Nearly every city block has a "No-tapiyc" (notary) office where papers, apparently, get stamped, copied, and processed. And then these stamped and processed papers get driven around the city where they get stamped, copied and processed again. It is the picture of activity-for-the-sake-of-activity. While sitting in traffic this afternoon, I wonder how many of our fellow drivers are either in route to a notary, or just came from one.

"Business does get done here," said an American business-man in Kiev earlier in the week. "It just doesn't get done quickly. They love their paperwork and their official stamps." It's become a running joke for us—on the way to the market we'll pretend to stop and get our grocery list notarized. But the joking is just a thinly veiled way of dealing with the frustration of a country that inexplicably makes well-intentioned families wait a long time and pay through the nose to adopt their orphans—the number of which is forever growing and too large to imagine.

Money is becoming a problem again as well. We're running low on cash, and in a few days will need to make a rent payment for the second half of our stay. We figure that it will be fairly easy to take our Visa or MasterCard down to one of the many ATMs in town, to pull out some cash. Wrong. Our cards don't work anywhere. Undeterred, we decide to take them into a large, Western-looking bank by our apartment to do a simple cash advance. Wrong again. "It's not possible," a thoroughly bored-looking teller explains. This phrase, "It's not possible," is possibly the most apt description of Ukrainian customer service and should probably be added to the national flag. We walk and drive around town to ten banks,[2] all of which say the same thing. We find one, finally, that is willing to release the completely random sum of $306 to us. This would leave us about $500 short, but at least would be a start. But when the teller swipes the card, she frowns at the little piece of paper spit out by the machine and says, you guessed it, "It's not possible."

At this point my blood pressure is through the roof, and I've probably worried years off my life. But this situation provides an opportunity for the body of Christ to come through again, this time via a friend from Kristin's expat women's Bible study. When she learns of our plight she puts us in touch with her husband, an influential American businessman in Kiev. He offers to pull the relatively small sum out of his account for us, and my parents generously offer to wire him the money (to an American account) the same day. We are struck by how literally and figuratively lost we would be without the church, and without this women's Bible study group, in Kiev. They have provided our social life here, and now, they're providing a means to get the money we need to pay our rent.

◇ ◇ ◇

Today we drive across town to pick up Dima's passport, and there it is, in print: Maximilian Dmitri Kluck. With each document this whole thing becomes more official. Once again, Dima is enthralled to be driving around town, pointing out "machinas" and "autobuses" in his husky little voice.

The buzzkill happens when we visit the Austrian Airlines office in Kiev, where we're told "There are no flights on Friday . . . no flights on Saturday . . . " and then told that we should "just go ahead and wait until the twentieth" which was the original date for our return ticket, and is two and a half weeks in the future. This, after we'd been told we could leave in a couple of days. The problem, ironically, is Easter. The celebration of Christ's resurrection is making it impossible for us to come home. Nice. It feels like there is a finish line, but unfortunately that finish line keeps getting moved.

We'll spend the evening on the phone with our travel agent, learning all about the massive fees that we'll have to pay to have any shot at getting out of here before the twentieth. And even so, there are no guarantees. I'm too angry to pray. I watch a few minutes of *The Boondock Saints* on my laptop, and then spend the majority of the night staring at the stupid, beveled ceiling. I hate this flat as much as I've ever hated anything in my life. I decide to stop staring at the bed for a little while, and instead stare out the window, where I see a rat run out from under the steps, to get a drink out of a mud puddle.

◌ ◌ ◌

The silver lining of course, in all of this, is Dima. He's a tiny boy—skin and bones—but he has a quick smile, and a warm embrace. He loves us—he loves being picked up, and held, and kissed. He's as tiny as Tristan is massive. In the stroller he just smiles and looks around—happy to take in the sights, sounds, and smells of a world he's missed out on up until this point. Our discipline problems with Tristan here have, in many ways, paralleled my own spiritual shortcomings in Kiev. If he's been whiny and petulant, I've been the same, just in a (sometimes) more appropriate, adult way. And God, thankfully, has gotten my attention and forced me into a closer, more sanctified, more joyful relationship with Him as a result. He has, at times, broken my will but not my spirit. This, I'm learning, is the role of a parent. My prayer is that Tristan will love God more and, honestly, love us more, as a result of the discipline. He's still my best buddy, and I love him dearly.

Dima's joy reminds me of the joy that's possible for us, in Christ, as His adopted heirs. It's a joy that has honestly mostly escaped me in life, but one that has literally been forced upon me here, as the other distractions[3] have been stripped away. I'm reminded, a little bit, of Paul sitting in prison, and feeling God's joy and presence in the midst of the nightmare that was, on paper, his life—a life that included imprisonment, beatings, and being misunderstood or outright rejected at every turn. Being misunderstood is a part of everyday life here.

But having Dima in our home, 24/7, is so infinitely better than visiting him at the orphanage. Just being able to feed him, to have him jump into our bed and cuddle when he wakes up in the morning, to be able to help him go potty—all of these little, mundane details are the exact things that bring us joy and allow us to feel like he's ours. He is ours. He is our son. I love that ours are the first faces he sees in the morning. These are all of the things that we loved, and still love, about raising Tristan.

I feel like Kristin and I have been to hell and back, twice, through all of this. Kiev is killing me, but she soldiers on, keeping it all together, and grows more beautiful to me by the day. I can't wait to get her home, to our house, so that we can just cuddle and laugh together again. She's my best friend, and I can't imagine life without her.

We stop at a park and Dima's thrilled to run around and kick a soccer ball with his brother and the Janzen kids. As I look at my two Ukrainian boys, now brothers and best friends; our new friends the Janzens, brothers and sisters in Christ; and the sunshine, I'm thankful. We are an American family.

NOTES

1. They all make me think of the Bob Balaban character in *Waiting for Guffman.*

2. After bank number six, the junky stroller that we overpaid for in Boyarka breaks in the middle of the street. One of the axles just shears in half. I swear and leave it on the sidewalk.

3. Read: comforts. Read: everything I like.

These people are so beautiful.
—Francis L. Whitman, *The Darjeeling Limited*

EPILOGUE

Typing this after returning from a blacktop soccer field outside our flat, where I ran into a handful of Ukrainian boys—probably middle-school-aged—who were enthralled with my American football and wanted to play catch. It was one of those "these people are beautiful" moments. The bravest of the boys, Mischa, approached me first—you could tell he was one of those tough, swaggery middle-school kids who matures faster than his friends and therefore has the most moxie in such situations. Mischa would drop back dramatically to throw the football and it would flutter, end over end, in my direction. This was in the evening, at the end of a beautiful, perfect spring day where the temperature topped out at about sixty-five degrees, and there was always a cool breeze blowing.

It's with this scene fresh in mind that I write about returning here, in a year, to adopt Dima's sister, Anastasia. She's a beautiful blonde-haired blue-eyed girl, age one year, who looks, as I've already mentioned, not unlike Cindy Lou Who from *How the Grinch Stole Christmas*. We were only allowed to see her twice, and each time just for a minute or two, but have committed to coming back to adopt her in a year, when she will be added to the official adoption registry.

The idea of coming back here both freaks me out and thrills me. This trip has been, in many ways, easier than the first. The adoption was smoother, and one would expect, it will be again with little Anastasia because the first step (her referral) is out of the way. In other ways it's been tougher, mainly due to the fact that we've grown soft[1] and spoiled by our suburban lives. I miss my comfy couch. My bed. My PlayStation. My carpet.

The potential challenges in Anastasia's adoption are many, namely, cost. We've gone into a significant amount of debt— but doable debt—to get the boys, and hadn't planned on adding a third $40,000 adoption into our budget. But when we were asked about Anastasia, we said "yes" after praying about it for a night. The Lord has provided for all of our needs, financially, even through some very lean writing years, and we know He'll be faithful to supply our needs in her case. But for the first time since a one-year stint as Campus Crusade missionaries a decade ago, we'll be raising money. This freaks us out, to say the least, namely because we just don't like asking people for things, but also because there were things about it (fundraising) that didn't sit well the first time. We're trusting God to smooth over the rough edges in this area.

Also scary is the fact that she'll be without us, in an orphanage, for at least another year. Please pray for her health, safety, and spiritual development during that year. We're sad to not be able to experience that year with her, but sadder still that it will be a year before we can begin to tell her the good news of Jesus Christ.

We were allowed to take two pictures of her, and we'll pray for her often as we look at her beautiful little face. And we'll pray that God will prepare us for what will be another difficult journey out of our respective comfort zones.

As my boys climb on me, smiling and laughing, I'm reminded of the fact that the difficult circumstances in their past, like abandonment, are, relatively speaking, washed away in light of the new life they have with our family. And I can't help but compare that to the regeneration that happens in our hearts, in Christ. We remember our old lives, but they pale in comparison to the joy that's possible in Him, and the glory we'll experience in eternity.

NOTE

1. It's worth noting here that I've grown softer, and more spoiled, than Kristin has. She never ceases to amaze me.

ACKNOWLEDGMENTS

Sitting here in the flat, in Kiev, looking at the first partly sunny day we've seen here in two weeks, I'm most thankful for our parents and families—and for the technology to keep in touch with them via Skype, email, and the blog. They've brightened my days, when things here were, quite literally and figuratively, grim. We're eternally grateful for their love, and for the gift of Christ that they shared with us when we were children. Thanks also to Kristin's brothers and their wives—Ryan and Kel, and Jeff and Catha—who have become not only siblings, but great friends to me.

A big thanks goes to our University Reformed Church family, and our friends Kevin and Trisha DeYoung. Thank you for your pastoral support and for being great friends. Thanks as well to everyone who read and commented on the blog. You have no idea how much it meant to see that our friends were thinking of us and cared enough to write. Thanks as well to Cory Hartman for the Skypes, chatting, pastoral wisdom, and friendship, and Chris Regner for the all-important NFL draft banter. Special thanks to Zach and Erin for always commenting, humorously, on the blog.

Huge thanks as well to Scott and Jen Shortenhaus, Jeff and Catha Skinner (and family), Aunt Linda, Ted and Karen Kluck, and the Shaohannah's Hope Foundation, Bonnie Skinner, and all who all made financial contributions to Tristan and Maxim's adoptions. We thank you from the bottom of our hearts for helping us become parents.

Special thanks as well to Judy Dalrymple, from Bethany Christian Services, for answering all of my snarky, passive-aggressive emails, and deciding when I was being legitimately concerned (sometimes), and when I was just being a wuss (often). Ditto for Jennifer Bryson, who has also been exceedingly kind and professional through our adoptions. Thanks to Lesya, Slava, Irina, Svetlana, and the rest of the staff in Ukraine for wonderful referrals. To Vadim for being a great driver who always followed traffic laws, liked speed limits and stop signs, and who was always eager to talk about rock music. To Bogdan for always getting us there a few minutes early, and for truly caring about the kids. And to Dr. Dubrovsky for running the whole show, as it were, though we've never actually met.

And a special paragraph goes to Milla and Sascha, in Simferopol, for their kindness and hospitality. We had a wonderful time in your home, and you made us feel comfortable and loved. God bless you both.

A huge thanks goes to Wes and Kim Janzen, as well as Johnny, Kristina, and CJ, for becoming great friends during our time in Kiev in spite of the fact that you were always making me climb to high places and then look down. You made our month and a half in Kiev not only bearable but fun, and your church was, quite literally, a God-send. It was the highlight of our weeks. Thanks as well to Kate and Sasha for a wonderful dinner, the Mulloolys for a great brunch, and the rest of the English-speaking expat community in Kiev for your kindness and hospitality during our stay.

Thank you to the Vinnitsa Wolves American football team for trekking to Kiev to talk football for the afternoon—and for graciously having me as a part of your team for a day. It brought me great joy to play my game in your country.

Thanks to Dr. Jami Newman and Dr. John Egger, stateside, for sending us to Ukraine well armed with antibiotics, and Dr. Egger in particular for helping us negotiate the endless requests for medical paperwork.

Thank you to Tristan's kindergarten teacher, Mrs. Promer, for being so understanding and cool about this and, just in general, for being such a great teacher. We appreciate what you and Mrs. Boyd do!

Thanks to Mark Mothersbaugh and Wes Anderson for the soundtracks to *The Royal Tenenbaums* and *The Life Aquatic with Steve Zissou*. Thank you to Cameron Crowe for everything about the movie *Almost Famous*. To Tom Hanks for doing *The Burbs* and *You've Got Mail* before becoming too serious for movies like these. Thanks as well to the late Dr. D. Martyn Lloyd-Jones for writing *Spiritual Depression*, a book that saved my emotional and spiritual bacon more than once during the second adoption.

And finally, thank you to the staff at Kofe Xaye in Kiev, for smiling frequently and not making us feel like idiots.

THE REASON FOR SPORTS

There are books on how to worship God with our marriages, our money, and our sex lives. Books on how to "think biblically" about movies, television, and the arts. Books on how to vote Christianly and how not to vote Christianly. But there is little thoughtful, Christ-centered writing on the subject that drives most of men's banter with each other and consumes the bulk of their free time. Sports.

Written in the vein of Rick Reilly (*Sports Illustrated*), Chuck Klosterman (*Spin, Esquire*), and David Foster Wallace (*A Supposedly Fun Thing I'll Never Do Again*), *The Reason for Sports* will both entertain and shed light on some of today's most pertinent sports issues: race, drugs, hero worship, and more—all through a biblical lens.

MOODY
PUBLISHERS
moodypublishers.com

WHY WE'RE NOT EMERGENT

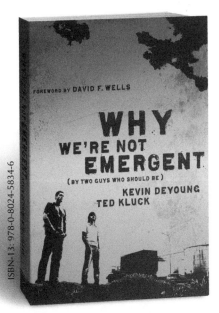

"You can be young, passionate about Jesus Christ, surrounded by diversity, engaged in a postmodern world, reared in evangelicalism, and not be an emergent Christian. In fact, I want to argue that it would be better if you weren't."

The emergent church is a strong voice in today's Christian community. And they're talking about good things: caring for the poor, peace for all mankind, loving Jesus. They're doing church a new way, not content to fit the mold. Again, all good. But there's more to the movement than that. Much more.

Kevin and Ted are two guys who, demographically, should be all over this movement. But they're not. And *Why We're Not Emergent* gives you the solid reasons why. From both a theological and an on-the-street perspective, Kevin and Ted diagnose the emerging church. They pull apart interviews, articles, books, and blogs, helping you see for yourself what it's all about.

MOODY
PUBLISHERS
moodypublishers.com

WHY WE LOVE THE CHURCH

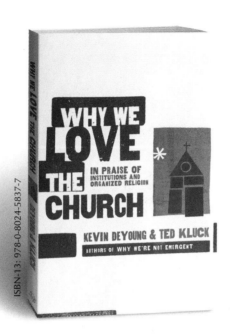

ISBN-13: 978-0-8024-5837-7

Authors Kevin DeYoung and Ted Kluck present the case for loving the local church. Their newest book paints a picture of the local church in all its biblical and real life guts, gaffes, and glory in an effort to edify local congregations and entice the disaffected back into the fold. It provides a solid biblical mandate to love and be part of the body of Christ and counteract the "leave church" books that trumpet rebellion and individual felt needs.

MOODY
PUBLISHERS
moodypublishers.com